Simple Pleasures *of* Friendship

Simple Pleasures *of*
Friendship

Celebrating the Ones We Love

Collected by
SUSANNAH SETON

CONARI PRESS

First published in 2004 by
Red Wheel/Weiser, LLC
York Beach, ME
With offices at:
368 Congress Street
Boston, MA 02210
www.redwheelweiser.com

Library of Congress Cataloging-in-Publication Data
Seton, Susannah.
Simple pleasures of friendship : celebrating the ones we love /
collected by Susannah Seton.
p. cm.
ISBN 1-57324-868-1
1. Friendship. I. Title.
BJ1533.F8S45 2004
177'.62—dc22
2003015356

Printed in the United States of America
RRD

11 10 09 08 07 06 05 04
8 7 6 5 4 3 2 1

The paper used in this publication meets the minimum requirements of the
American National Standard for Information Sciences–Permanence of Paper for
Printed Library Materials z39.48–1992 (r1997).

Friendship is a word the very sight
of which in print makes the heart warm.

—Augustine Birrell

Simple Pleasures *of*
Friendship

Acknowledgments xi

Indelibly Etched in Our Hearts xiii

ACKNOWLEDGMENTS

A big thank you to all those who contributed stories to this collection, especially Kathy Cordova, for roping in all her writer friends and helping spread the word. Our friendship is new, but precious nonetheless.

A bow of appreciation to my dear friend Mary Beth Sammons for writerly support over the years and permission to excerpt from her wonderful book *Gifts with Heart,* copyright © 2002 by Mary Beth Sammons. Reprinted by permission of Conari Press.

Mega-thanks to my editor, Jan Johnson, who had the idea for this book in the first place.

Thanks to Annette Madden for typing assistance and friendship inspiration.

Indelibly Etched in Our Hearts

The real test of friendship is.... Can you
enjoy together those moments of life that
are utterly simple? They are the moments
people look back on at the end of life
and number as their most
sacred experiences.

—Eugene Kennedy

What is it about friends that is so special? Why out of all the
people we come across in our lives do we form attachments to
certain folks, attachments so strong that even the thought of
them brings a smile to our faces? Each of us has his or her own
answer to those questions, but no matter how we understand

the connection, there's no doubt that our friendships play a huge part in making our lives worth living.

For years now, I have been collecting stories of ordinary people's simple pleasures, the homey little things that give life its zest—a hot bath, the first smell of lilacs in spring, the sight of grey and black juncos against a snowdrift. I've looked at what gives us delight inside our homes and outside in our gardens. I've asked folks to share what traditions give holidays their special meaning. In three books, I have explored the pleasures of the material world that we can have at low or no cost, encouraging us all to consider how to fold more joy and comfort into our daily lives.

This book is different. It is a celebration, not of the world of objects, but of the pleasures of the most precious gift any person can ever receive: friendship.

What are the simple pleasures of friendship? That's what I set out to discover and commemorate when I sent out a notice to writers' groups around the world, asking for contributions. I received contributions from South Africa and Australia, Mexico, Malaysia, India, England, and all fifty of the United States. Contributors ranged in age from a twelve year old to folks in their seventies.

Reading the hundreds of submissions, I quickly saw themes: in particular, the satisfaction of staying in touch across time and space (there were dozens of stories about the joys of e-mail and long-distance phone calls) and the joys of unlikely friendship between people seemingly very different (I could have filled an entire book with intergenerational friendship stories alone). There was the happiness of reuniting after a long time, on the one hand, and of daily contact on the other. There was the pleasure of life-long connection and the delight of the briefest encounter. All are celebrated moments in time—large or small—with one friend or many who are indelibly etched in their hearts.

Overall, three common threads emerged: friends bring us the pleasure of play by joining us in life's fun adventures. They bring us the pleasure of comfort by being there in times of trouble. And they bring us the pleasure of understanding, as they witness the unfolding of our lives over time. So that's how the book is organized.

It is my hope that in reading these stories, you will experience double pleasure: first at the warm feelings the authors express toward their friends, and second at your memories of similar times with your own. And because my guess is that the stories will prompt you to reach out to the friends in your life, I also offer dozens of easy-to-make gifts and recipes to share with the special folks who make up your friendship circle.

Friendship is truly one of life's simple pleasures. No amount of money can purchase it. We can't fake it—we either feel it or not. We can't make it happen. We experience it by being ourselves, in communion with others being themselves—people whom we feel a special connection to. Simple? Yes, but mysterious and profound, too.

May this book help you remember the joy that friendship brings you, may it help you forge even stronger bonds to those you count as friends, and may your life always be filled with the pleasure of good friends.

—Susannah Seton

FUN AND FROLIC

Grief can take care of itself, but to get the full value
of joy you must have somebody
to divide it with.

—MARK TWAIN

Friends are the folks we *play* with, as kids and as adults. Our adventures together give life its zest, even if we are doing nothing more than sitting around together sharing a meal or a movie. And watch out when we really get going!

_____

Shop 'til We Drop

What is it about shopping that cements a friendship between women? Perhaps it's the shared time browsing together, enjoying the splash of colors, fingering the smooth silk or the nubby tweed, while the scents of perfume from the exotic to the floral drift through the stores. Maybe it's the idea of the quest, the search for the perfect black dress or the pursuit of a bargain, with the malls and stores becoming giant treasure chests filled with wonderful and exotic discoveries.

As a teenager, I'd hit the mall with my friends. We were a giggling pack of self-conscious hormones. We tried on dresses, then outrageous, floppy hats that we'd never buy, always keeping an eye out for any cute boys.

Now I'm a mom. I park my stroller at the mall playground and catch up with my friends in between shopping forays. We compare childhood developmental notes, trade discipline strategies, and laugh over silly things our kids say, while the mall fountain ripples in the background.

More than anything, I think we shop together because it mirrors our relationships. Men play golf; they compete. Women stroll between crowded racks and weave in and out among display cases, with conversations meandering with their steps. Our casual chitchat can dip unexpectedly into private pain and confidences over a rack of shirts or in front of the three-way dressing room mirror. Our conversations crisscross, our paths wind through unexpected turns, while our lives intertwine in deeper friendship.

—*Sara E. Rosett*

And in the sweetness of friendship
let there be laughter, and sharing of
pleasures. For in the dew of little
things the heart finds its morning
and is refreshed.

—Kahlil Gibran

Personalized Wrapping Paper

After you've shopped your heart out for a gift for a friend, consider adding a special touch with your very own wrapping paper. Or give the paper itself as a gift. You'll need solid color wrapping paper, small cookie cutters, and heavy-body acrylic paint (available at art supply stores). Lay out the wrapping paper. Dip the cutting edge of the cookie cutter into the paint and stamp onto the paper, beginning at the top left-hand corner. Thin the paint with water if it's too lumpy. Continue until you've covered all the paper. Shapes can line up or overlap, depending on the design you've chosen. Allow to dry thoroughly before using.

You've Got Mail

When I was younger, I thought friendship meant constantly being together, doing each other's hair and nails, and talking about boys on the phone. I'm twenty-five now and have moved around a lot in the past years because of my job. As a result, deep and lasting relationships have been scarce. Thanks to the modern technology of e-mail, however, I have friendships all over the world.

My friend in Germany sends me recipes she thinks even I would be able to follow. My friend in Brazil can find anything about anyone on the net, which comes in handy when I'm looking for the latest news on my favorite French actor. An artist buddy scans all her work and mails it to me before putting it forward to the various galleries, so that I can have my say—which is always good, of course. If I lived in New York, I would be the first in line to her show, to say so.

I reply with news about my day, about the comings and goings of life in South Africa, and the status of my seemingly never-to-be-finished novel, which I don't have time for. I scour the Sunday papers for interesting tidbits of information that any of them might find remotely useful.

Thanks to that little voice crying, "You have mail," I live in a city with millions of people that I don't know, yet I never feel lonely. There's one other advantage. No matter how many times you move, one address remains the same. Your e-mail address.

—*Liana van Niekerk*

The world is so empty if one thinks
only of mountains, rivers and cities; but
to know someone who thinks and feels
with us, and who, though distant is close
to us in spirit, this makes the earth
for us an inhabited garden.

—GOETHE

The Girls on the Second Floor

Everyone in the apartment complex knew us, the girls on the second floor, by the sounds of rolling luggage at all hours of the day and night, by the slamming of trunks and car doors echoing off the buildings, by a car starting and then speeding off toward the Baltimore/Washington International Airport.

The four of us were in our twenties, just starting out as flight attendants. We all had pagers on our hips and an ear out for the phone. Bored and restless, we would wait for scheduling to call, passing books from one to another to help the reserve days go by quickly. Scary movies were another favorite pastime. We would sit on our futon couch, scrunched up together in the dark, eating popcorn. At some point one of us would always scream, causing a chain reaction. But we always ended up doubled over in laughter.

When one of us finally received "the call," we would scurry around the two-bedroom apartment, throwing makeup, hairspray, and travel necessities in the chosen one's suitcase. She'd put her uniform on, touch up her makeup, and pin on her wings. With a final look in the mirror, she would be out the door.

Whoever was left behind was responsible for making sure the Friday night parties happened. The music started out soft, with just a few friends present. As the evening progressed, however, the music grew louder and the apartment teemed with people. Finally a broomstick would pound on our living-room floor from the apartment below, which led to a formal apology the next day.

On weekend mornings, we received a wakeup call from Navy planes flying over our apartment. The planes appeared so close that it seemed as if we could touch them if we stood on a ladder. We would climb out of bed, drink our coffee, and talk about the night before. Eventually, we would get ready for the day. By late afternoon we were found wandering the brick streets of Annapolis, admiring the old homes that graced the historical area. We attended Navy football games when it was a home game, and made our presence known at the local pubs later on.

On mellow evenings, we would gather with a bottle of white zinfandel and chat on our apartment balcony, Tracy Chapman's song "The Promise" playing in the background. Sometimes we resolved an argument. Other times, we dreamed about our weddings, having babies, whether or not the guys in our lives were "the one." We talked about the rude passenger that yelled at us, or the man who passed out in our galley. Sometimes we shared a pack of cigarettes, at other times a box of Kleenex.

Now, years later, the idea of having roommates makes me cringe. Still, I treasure the memories of dancing in the living room and the pictures of us in downtown Annapolis. Every fall I search for a certain candle that smells like the candy corn we burned in those days. It never fails to bring me back to the living room in that second-floor apartment.

—*Elizabeth L. Blair*

A joy shared is a joy doubled.

—GOETHE

Parmesan Popcorn

You don't have to live together to have a movie night. Why not call a few friends, pick a theme (scary, romantic, top favorites), rent a few videos or DVDs, and try this popcorn recipe? It's much tastier than the packaged kind, and unbelievably easy to make. The flavored salt gives it even more of a distinctive flavor.

> 2 teaspoons cooking oil
> ¼ cup unpopped popcorn
> ¼ cup melted butter
> ½ cup grated Parmesan cheese
> salt, garlic salt, or celery salt, to taste

Put the oil and popcorn in a popcorn popper and pop until done. Combine remaining ingredients in a mixing cup and pour over popcorn. Stir well and serve. Makes 2 quarts.

Divine Intervention

Our house had been on the market for six months, and there was still no buyer. What if we never sold it? The new house would be ready in eight weeks, and then what would we do? Two houses, two mortgages! It didn't bear thinking about.

Besides, I was fed up keeping the place so *clean*. The flower arrangements insisted upon by the real estate agent made it look and smell more like a funeral parlor than a house. The scent of Lysol overlaid with chrysanthemum was a stench reminiscent of decay. I needed to kvetch, so I called Eileen. "I've got just the thing," she said, after hearing of my dilemma. "I'll be right there."

I sighed. "She's probably bringing over another set of curtains," I decided. She'd loaned me the ones in the spare bedroom— the previous set having been described by our agent as "a bit too sixtyish." I wondered at the time whether possessing an attitude of disdain was a prerequisite for a job in real estate. In any event, I was sure it was going to take more than better curtains to sell this house.

Eileen was there in an hour, waving what looked like a white plastic toy in my face. "I could have given you lunch," I said, slightly annoyed. I thought she'd gotten the toy free with burger and fries.

"Look," she said. "I've brought St. Joseph. We'll bury him in the backyard, and then your house will sell. Come on, where

do you want to put him? He has to be upside down or it won't work."

Had she lost her mind? I knew Eileen was religious, but this was ridiculous. My own grandmother had been institutionalized once with something called "religious mania." Could my friend be going the same way? Should I humor her?

"Eileen," I spluttered. "I don't think saints do things for Jews, do they?"

"St. Joseph's flexible."

I just looked at her.

"It might not work," she said. "But I've heard of people it has worked for."

"But you don't actually *know* any, do you?"

"Well . . . no . . . but . . ." She giggled.

I began to giggle too.

Laughing, we went out back, dug a hole, and plunked the plastic figurine into it, upside down of course. I hoped the neighbors weren't watching.

I was still smiling as I said goodbye to Eileen. The sheer ridiculousness of the adventure had made me feel better. Eileen was the best kind of friend, and if St. Joseph had to be part of the deal, so be it. But it would take more than a statue to sell the house.

The house sold the following day.

—*Margaret Davidson*

Celebrate the happiness that friends
are always giving,
make every day a holiday and
celebrate just living!

—AMANDA BRADLEY

Partners in Crime

Fighting back tears, I watched one of my best friends walk down the aisle. While I was incredibly happy for Molly, memories of us goofing around when we were younger made me long for times past. That morning, her cousin had presented her with an album of pictures and stories of her premarriage life. We had all submitted something. As Molly neared the altar, I thought of my contribution to her album—a picture of the two of us at fourteen playing our French horns.

Molly and I met in junior high band. At the beginning of band, our conductor would tune the different instruments separately and then tune us all together. The French horn has a thumb key. When depressed, the thumb key can completely change any note you play. Molly and I thought it was funny to depress the thumb key when the whole band was tuning on the same note.

Our conductor, Mr. Timber, would make a little wrinkle in his forehead, trying to locate the source of the horribly out-of-tune sound. At first, he couldn't pinpoint that it was us, so he would have to go back and tune each instrument separately, as we concealed our grins.

As time went by, Mr. Timber caught on to our little game. One day, as we began giggling after an episode of tuning, he marched briskly toward us, pointed two fingers—one at each of us—and barked, "You two!" Then he proceeded to go into the next room, indicating that we were to follow him. We exchanged a scared look and went out after him.

To this day, I have no idea what Mr. Timber said in those five minutes. I was just concentrating on not smiling. I knew that if I smiled I would make the situation worse. I also knew that if I gave Molly a sideways glance, it would set us into a fit of uncontrollable laughter. This was very difficult since we were also both trying to avoid Mr. Timber's bad breath. We were trying not to breathe, trying not to look at each other, and trying not to crack a smile.

Now, at twenty-five, it is something we both still laugh about—and laughing together is the best thing to do with a friend. When you can laugh at yourself, you can handle anything. Realizing that, I knew Molly would find happiness in her new marriage and that we could always count on each other for a good laugh.

—*Amanda Seim*

A friend is another self.

—ARISTOTLE

Served with Love

I opened my blue cookbook a few days ago to look for a recipe that a friend gave me. Where was that recipe for ice cream pie that my neighbor Kim made for my husband's birthday? She filled a crushed Oreo cookie crust with softened ice cream, then topped it with drizzled chocolate syrup. Oh, there it was, folded into my copy of *Joy of Cooking*, along with a well-creased paper, an e-mail from a friend at work, with the recipe for her easy and wonderful Christmas fudge.

That got me to thinking about all the food I've shared with friends: a creamy alfredo noodle dish from Bev, the chicken pasta salad another friend made for me when I was pregnant and my husband was out of town. I still make that pasta salad, and every time I toss the chicken, noodles, carrots, cucumbers, cheese, and dressing, I remember our relaxed conversation while I set her table and then perched on a chair while she pulled warm rolls from her oven. Food's pleasures are doubled when shared.

—*Sara E. Rosett*

Friendships, like geraniums,
bloom in kitchens.

—BLANCHE H. GELFANT

Personalized Cookbooks

It started out for me. I was struggling to figure out how to deal with all the recipes I clipped out of the food magazines I love so much. I ended up buying a blank book and pasting the recipes inside. I filled two huge books that way before I realized that it was not the most efficient way to collect such things: "Hmm, I'd like to make that braised raddiccio. It was somewhere on a left-hand page in the middle of the book with the blue cover. . . ."

So when my friend Diane asked me for the recipe for something she had eaten at my house, I decided to make her a personalized cookbook like mine—only better. This one would have sections—Appetizers, Soups, Entrees, Side Dishes, Desserts—and be in a three-ring binder so that she could add to it in the appropriate sections. I would start her off with all the things she had eaten at my house that she liked, and she could take it from there. She loved it—and soon I was making ones for all my friends. Not only did they enjoy their books, but I get a kick every time I go to one of their houses and see my cookbook on the counter, covered with cooking stains! There's no higher compliment to a chef than imitation.

Into the Pool

Meeting Debbie when I was thirty-three was like meeting a new playmate during second-grade recess and knowing we'd be "best friends." Only it didn't happen on the playground. It happened in the predawn hours of a September morning after Debbie and I had swum the first 600 yards of a workout with our Masters swim team.

Two thousand yards and a dozen fifteen-second conversations later (the out-of-breath moments between swim sets), we had already shared some hearty laughs. During the kicking set near the end of the workout, we finally held a longer chat; the kick boards allowed us to keep our heads above water and swim side by side.

We learned that we were both one year postpartum, that her baby daughter and my twin girls were born only three days apart, and that her older daughter and my son were only a year apart. We were both still hauling around an extra fifteen pregnancy pounds, and we were stay-at-home moms who were held prisoner in our homes with young children during the day, and hence could only swim the morning practice. By the time we finished the workout and darted for our cars to get home before our husbands left for work, Debbie had convinced me to come swim with her every Monday, Wednesday, and Friday.

Soon thereafter we introduced our children to each other and set up frequent play dates. Within weeks we became each other's confidante. By the end of the year, we were so much in synch that we could laugh our way through monthly bouts of PMS at the same time! In just over a year, we have swum in ten open-water races together, including a relay across Lake Tahoe and an insane adventure jumping off a ferry boat, with 400 other swimmers, into the 58-degree San Francisco Bay—without wet suits—to race to Alcatraz Island.

Out of the water, we've watched our little girls, now two years old, develop a sweet friendship, and our older children become playmates. We've watched one another shrink two sizes of jeans into the swimmers' bodies we flaunted as teenagers—or at least before motherhood. Our friendship was born in the water but thrives on land. Another added benefit? With our mutual motivation to keep each other in the pool, we'll both always fit into our size 6's!

—*Cameron Sullivan*

To like and dislike the same things, that is
indeed true friendship.

—Sallust

Natural Skin Cream

After a swim, skin needs some pampering. This cream lasts
about one month at room temperature, and can be refrigerated
for longer life. Beeswax is available at craft and health stores. If
you want it to be a shade other than white, add a few drops of
food coloring at the same time as the oils.

8 teaspoons almond oil

¼ cup grated beeswax

8 teaspoons distilled water

16 drops of your favorite essential oil

Place the almond oil and beeswax in the top of a double
boiler. Heat until wax melts, stirring frequently. Remove from
heat, whisk in water and essential oil to emulsify the cream.
Immediately turn into a sterilized container with a tight-fitting
lid. Makes approximately ½ cup.

Finding Essential Oils and Other Supplies

Good sources for essential oils and other aromatherapy products are Bare Escentuals (800-227-3990), The Body Shop by Mail (800-541-2535), and Inner Balance catalog (800-345-3371). There are also many great sites online, including *butterburandsage.com*, *buyaromatherapy.com*, and *aromaproducts.com*.

Childhood Memory

Sitting on the front steps of my best friend Pat's house those many years ago, the August sun resting on our tan shoulders, we decided that, Akron, Ohio, was the hottest place on earth. Desperate for a breeze, we brought our bicycles into the shade of the porch and flipped them upside down. Balancing the bikes on their handlebars, we operated the pedals by hand and spun the rear wheels as fast as possible. One thing led to another, and soon our makeshift fans became massive props pushing a frigate through high seas toward a beleaguered aircraft carrier (the neighbor's garage). Broom handles shoved through the rubberized bands of complexly folded chaise lounge chairs became antiaircraft guns, and Pat's little sister's tricycle became the helm.

The carrier was sinking fast, and the enemy was shooting at the sailors in the water. There was no way to reach them in time! Pat and I looked over our hopelessly underpowered engines and then at each other. There was only one solution. Acknowledging the inherent risks of using experimental technology in a battle situation, we formed a pact of secrecy, gave the official Navy handshake, and agreed that desperate times required desperate measures. Then we commandeered his big brother's new ten-speed.

With one of us operating the gears and the other cranking

the pedals, we were able to achieve a cooling breeze and, with the addition of a baseball card held in place by a clothespin, nearly warp speed. Our frigate hydroplaned across the water to the rescue. I dove across the deck to the antiaircraft gun and began picking off enemy fighters. The choppy seas made sighting difficult, and the engine became unstable on its tiny handlebars. A fighter crashed into the water just a few feet from the bow, and the explosion sent me backwards into Pat, who in turn fell into the engine compartment.

What followed was a sickening KaCHUNK! Pat and I looked at one another in horror; we had sustained heavy damage. The rear derailer of our ten-speed engine was jammed and the chain contorted into a pretzel. We were dead in the water. Enemy aircraft threatened to turn us into Swiss cheese, and Pat's brother was due home any minute! Pat ran below deck and returned with a screwdriver. I leaned on the tension pulley and slacked the chain, while Pat pried the links from between the axle and the rear sprocket. We spun the pedal, and the gears engaged just as Pat's brother appeared around the corner at the end of the street. We quickly put the ten-speed back where we found it, powered up the old engines, and proceeded to save the crew and dispatch the enemy.

If not for the exceptional skill and sacrifice of Chief Engineer Pat, and myself as Gunner's Mate, the world would surely have ended. Needless to say, the ice-cream man was very impressed and listened with interest while mooring his supply vessel along our starboard bow.

—*Michael S. McKlusky*

Are we not like the two volumes
of one book?

—Marceline Desbordes-Valmore

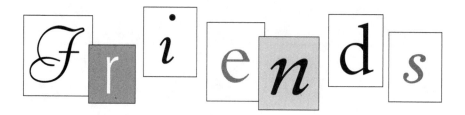

Playing for Keeps

Sometimes when you meet someone, you just know right away that you are going to be friends. That's what happened with Carrie and me. I had taken a temporary job at the place where Carrie worked, and Carrie was the first person I met there. From the minute we met, we got along fine.

We soon discovered we both have the same abiding passion— we love to play Scrabble. We began to have all-day Scrabble marathons, usually at her house. Carrie's husband and children got used to the sight of the two of us sitting at her dining room table with the Scrabble board between us, concentrating on making words out of our letters. We did it so often that after a while her husband, Mike, would ask her, "Is Conover coming over to play Scrabble today?"

After a while Carrie and I got bored with regular Scrabble. So we began to experiment with longer words and bigger scores. Then we moved on to using names of associations and titles of songs. Ever supportive, Mike bought us two new Scrabble games, because Carrie and I kept running out of letters. Now we go online and search for the longest names of whatever we can find. We each have our own board, and we keep all the letters face up between us, so we can find what we want more easily. We wrap our words around the board. So far, Carrie has had the longest phrase. It was a title to a magazine article, and it took up all her board and one line on mine. She made three hundred billion points. (We have our own scoring method, too.)

Carrie and I so enjoy our way of playing that we've named it "C and C Scrabble." Whoever we tell about how we play usually tells us we can't play that way, that we're cheating. But we just shrug and reply that it isn't cheating if we make up our own rules. Mike said it best when he said, "It makes you happy and that's all that matters."

And that's true about our friendship, too. It makes us happy and that's all that matters.

—*Conover Swofford*

Friendship is a magic weaver.

—PROVERB

Friendship Code

When I say that no one understands me as well as my best friend, I mean that literally. Over the years, we've developed a kind of secret code, a friendship shorthand. It started accidentally when she wanted to go to a certain coffeehouse, but couldn't remember the name. So she used the name of a similar-looking place in our former college town. Not only did I know the place she was referring to, but we've called it by its secret name for so long that I can no longer remember its correct name. Then I began having trouble with my boss, who actually forbid us to smile on the job. (The theory being that if we had time to smile, we weren't being efficient.) From that point on, he became "Mr. Nofun."

In our code, the past often mixes with the present as we refer to a colleague's clever actions as "pulling a Julie," or describe a gaudy piece of jewelry as "Bonniefied." We recall shared memories with just a few words: "chicken dinner in Mexico" makes us laugh, while mentioning "Fourth of July, 1986" casts a somber mood. Anyone eavesdropping on us would have difficulty deciphering our conversation.

That's why we only do this when we're alone. Talking this way in front of others misses the point. It's not to keep other people out; it's to keep us in.

—*Michelle Mach*

'Tis the privilege of friendship to
talk nonsense, and have her
nonsense respected.

—CHARLES LAMB

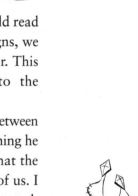

Automobile Adventure

It was the seventies, and my friend and I were
adventuring through the heart of Germany in a
rented VW "Beetle" with standard floor shift.
Because I was used to an automatic transmission but could read
German, and she could drive the car but not read the signs, we
decided that she would be the driver and I the navigator. This
worked well getting us out of Frankfurt and onto the
Autobahn.

Traveling north on the Autobahn, we got sandwiched between
two large trucks. The driver behind us waved, and, assuming he
was being friendly, we waved back. My friend asked what the
two large words were on the back of the truck in front of us. I
started going through my German dictionary, when the first truck
turned onto a side road. We were too close to do anything but
follow, the second truck close behind. "Verboten," the dictionary
informed me, meant "forbidden." I rapidly turned pages until I

found the second word, "Dynamit" which, as you might be able to guess, means "dynamite."

The trucks were heading for a nearby quarry to blast rock. Finally the truck behind slowed enough for us to pull over to the side of the road. As he passed, we could see he was laughing uproariously. Sheepishly, we turned around and went back to the Autobahn. So much for instant language interpretation. I was admittedly rattled, but managed to get us to our destination an hour late. It was then I discovered I'd had the map upside down.

My friend was still my friend—and still is—even though, as she puts it laughingly even now, "You will follow anyone, anywhere."

—*Marie Asner*

We cherish our friends not for their
ability to amuse us, but for ours
to amuse them.

—Evelyn Waugh

Haul Out the Photo Albums

The older the better. Look at yourself and friends in those funny clothes and haircuts. Remember that shack the two of you used to live in? The trip to the Florida Keys you took in college, when you ate grapefruits off trees and slept on the beach? That old Mustang he used to drive? There's great pleasure in reminiscing, and photos are a great way to reconnect to the past. Take a trip through your friendship yesterdays—preferably together.

Reality Barometer

One of the true joys of friendship is having someone who promises to tell you when:

Your hair looks horrible

You look like a tramp in that dress

Your butt looks huge in those pants

That color doesn't flatter

You definitely need a face lift

You definitely need to stop having face lifts

It's time to get out of those skin-tight leather pants and into something more age-appropriate before you end up looking like Cher.

On second thought, maybe lying's better.

Honesty may be the best policy, but it's
important to remember that apparently,
by elimination, dishonesty is the
second-best policy.

—GEORGE CARLIN

Walkabout

I've been trying to lose weight for years. I know it requires exercise, but I *so* hate to do it. I just could never stick to any regimen I started. That's why I was thrilled when a neighbor down the street asked me, a few years ago, if I wanted to walk each morning around the lake near our houses. I barely knew Sally, but I was desperate for a solution to my exercise dilemma. How could I not do it with her showing up at my door at seven a.m., dog leash in hand and monstrous poodle in tow?

That was three years ago, and now I wouldn't dream of missing a day. Snowstorms, rain, the heat of summer, we're out there, walking and talking. We gossip, laugh, chitchat about our dogs and those of the other walkers. We try to see how fast we can go. The time goes flying by.

Such a simple thing—a forty-five-minute walk with a friend. But the lift it gives me each morning sets the tone for my day.

—*Elizabeth Gonzales*

But friendship is precious,
not only in the shade, but in the
sunshine of life; and thanks to a
benevolent arrangement of things, the
greater part of life is sunshine.

—THOMAS JEFFERSON

Peppermint Foot Bath

After a brisk walk, surprise your friend with this relaxing foot bath.

> nonaluminum saucepan with lid
>
> 5 cups water
>
> 4 ounces dried peppermint leaves
>
> 8 ounces juniper berries (available at grocery stores)
>
> 24 drops sandalwood essential oil
>
> 12 drops cypress essential oil
>
> 1 coffee filter
>
> funnel
>
> pretty bottles or small jars with lids
>
> labels and ribbon

Place the water in the pan. Add the peppermint and juniper and heat on medium low to just below boiling point, stirring occasionally. Remove from heat, cover, and allow to cool. Add the essential oils and stir well.

Place the filter in the funnel and strain off the liquid into the bottles. To use, fill a large pan with hot water, stir in ¼ of a bottle, and soak feet for ten minutes.

The Poker Boys

On the first Friday of every month, five friends and I get together at one of our houses to play poker. But first we eat. The host prepares dinner, and because the chef job rotates to each of us only twice a year, we all try to outdo each other in culinary excess. When it's my turn, I pore over *Saveur* and raid my wife's cookbooks. I've made gumbo that requires stirring the roux for one hour until it turns exactly the right shade of brown, paella with six kinds of shellfish, Italian pork loin braised in milk—if it's full of saturated fat and carbohydrates, I've dished it up.

The first hour we eat and catch up on one another's lives—what's happening at work, who's bought a house, how the landscaping's going. Then the game begins—serious card playing that never seems to end until two a.m. no matter when we call last round. (We do take a dessert break at around eleven; wouldn't want to get hungry, after all.) The stakes are low—the most anyone has ever won in an evening is $40, but we hoot and holler nonetheless. We even have a trophy that rotates to the winner of the evening; at the end of the year, it gets engraved with the name of the guy who won the most that year. Sometimes someone can't make it, but that's rare, and if he hasn't given advance notice of at least a week, he gets fined $20.

Nothing fancy, but I love it. It's the one opportunity in the month that I get to let off steam with the guys. We must all appreciate the chance—the six of us began playing almost twenty years ago, right out of college. We're still at it—through marriages, moves, babies, job changes. Depending on who's hosting, we may end up driving over an hour to get there. A few other men have come and gone, but the six of us play on.

—*Donald McIlraith*

The feeling of friendship is like that of being comfortably filled with roast beef.

—Samuel Johnson

Poker-Night Flank Steak

Here's a recipe that has been a huge favorite among the poker-playing friends. Try it the next time you have hearty meat-eating friends over for a barbeque.

¼ cup low-sodium soy sauce

¼ cup Worcestershire sauce

2 tablespoons grated fresh ginger

2 tablespoons freshly squeezed lemon juice

2 cloves garlic, minced

pepper to taste

1½ pounds flank steak, trimmed

Combine all ingredients except steak in a dish large enough to hold the steak. Place steak in dish, turning over several times to coat. Cover and refrigerate overnight, turning once or twice.

Prepare a grill to high heat. Remove steak from pan, reserving marinade. Grill the steak for 4 minutes per side until medium rare. Slice diagonally into ¼-inch thick slices and place on serving platter. Heat the marinade in the microwave until boiling, then serve on the side. Serves 4.

Listening to Leaves

At the end of the day, before the sun goes down, we go and listen to the leaves. Just Luka and me.

The wind pushes against us, ruffling our hair. Wind chimes swing wildly. We walk faster past garages, windows, and doorways. Leaves rattle sideways, tripping over our toes. A robin clings to the top of a swaying branch.

We stop under a tree. This is the perfect spot. I whisper to Luka, "If you are patient and very, very still, so still you are hardly breathing, you can hear the leaves sing." We wait and we listen, trying hard not to breathe.

In-between the bird song and gentle insect scuttles, the leaves take up a rustle and pass it on. One by one, cluster by cluster, branch by branch, until a soft song ripples through the tree.

The wind swirls, whisking leaves to whirling delight. Leafsong echoes the galloping wind, soaring into the sky. Rising, roaring a crescendo of harmony. Fading to a murmur, a gasp. Silence.

A few weary leaves twist, sigh, and spin to the ground. Luka and I catch them as they fall, russet, golden and crunchy. We chase them, fall over each other, laughing. Then we throw the leaves—up, up—until we are covered in autumn.

A scruffy cat slinks from under a bridge, stops, stares, then mooches on by. The light is fading. Time to go.

We jiggle as we walk. Back past the dented garage door. Past the soggy tennis ball abandoned on a sunnier day. Up the steps,

through the leaves, to our front door.

Luka and I stop to watch the sun go down. The wind has died. A faint aroma of wood smoke hangs in the air. I squeeze Luka's hand. He squeezes back. Tomorrow we will listen to the leaves again.

Just Luka and me.

—*Keely James*

Life is to be fortified by many friendships.
To love and to be loved is the greatest
happiness of existence.

—Sydney Smith

The Reunion

I sat motionless on the toilet in a stall in the ladies' room of the York County Elks Club. Dropping my head back, I dabbed at my throat with a fresh wad of toilet paper. I'd forgotten how hot it could get in June. "And you had to go and pick black lace," I thought.

I grabbed my thick, curly dark hair, bunching it on top of my head so that I could wipe the back of my neck. But I remembered the frizz problem, and let the hair fall back to my shoulders.

The neighboring toilet flushed, and I bent down to watch silver-clad feet walk out of the stall. I inspected my own shoes—black, strappy pumps, peau de soie, with the year's highest acceptable heel. I shifted on the toilet seat and waited. I breathed slowly through my mouth, eyes closed, wondering who was washing and drying her hands out there.

Finally heels clicked across the tiled floor. The bathroom door swung open, letting in a rush of music from the Elks Club meeting hall. Old Motown, I realized. Of course. The door closed, the music receded, and I was alone.

No one had seen me yet. "You could still leave," I told myself, opening the stall door and peeking out. I walked to the mirror. I ran my hands down the sides of the dress, feeling my ribcage. I pinched my waist, and feeling no extra skin, patted my hips. Nothing shook. "Tank," I whispered, wincing a bit, remembering the hateful nickname I had been stuck with in high school. I hoped twenty fewer pounds and twenty years were enough. I took one more look at my slimmed-down figure, checked my lipstick, and walked out of the bathroom.

I stood in the doorway. The room was crowded, with people bunched into tight groups, talking and laughing loudly over the music. I recognized most of the faces, and smiled at each faintly, but couldn't make myself enter the room.

"Tank!" I wasn't certain that I'd heard it at first, thinking, hoping it might be the music. But the voice came again, louder: "Tank!" I turned, and there she was. Kathy. The cheerleader, the beauty queen. All blue eyes, straight blond hair. Still. "Why, Darsey, you haven't changed a bit. Everyone's over there," she said, pointing to the gaggle of her buddies. "You just HAVE to come over." She smiled stiffly, all teeth, then turned around, leaving a wake of perfume. I watched her walk away.

"Look at them. They're all hanging together. Just like the old days. And you know why Kathy's wearing that outfit don't you?"

I wheeled around, coming almost nose to nose with Joy. Joy, glowing, in a black lace dress and silver high-heeled shoes, laughed with delight. I laughed too, and answered, "No. Why?"

"Because she's hiding twenty pounds, that's why." Joy held out her arms.

"Joy!" I said, and hugged my old friend.

—Darsey Hamilton

Laughter is inner jogging.

—NORMAN COUSINS

Adult Dress-Up

My friend Daphne and I love to play dress-up. We go shopping just for fun and spend a few hours trying on clothes. Ball gowns are particularly enjoyable. Just the other day we found the perfect thing for her to wear to the Academy Awards, if she were ever invited. She looked just like Marilyn Monroe at JFK's birthday party. Our favorite location for such frolics is Loehmann's because they have a group dressing room, so we have plenty of room to maneuver. We've played dress-up with fur coats, outrageous hats, death-defying high heels. All of the pleasure with none of the cost (well, sometimes we look so divine we can't help opening up the old wallet, and there *was* that time when Daphne left with ten smashing dresses . . .).

—*M. J. Ryan*

Friendship is the wine of life.

—EDWARD YOUNG

Play Date

How about calling up a friend for a play date? Who says such events have to be only for kids? Adults need playtime too. How do you and your friend like to play? A day at the spa? A game of tennis followed by a good chat? Picnic in the park? Rather than feeling guilty that you don't spend enough time with friends, create an event.

How about a picnic for a change of pace? Here are two easy-to-make dishes. Add some cookies and drinks, and you are all set.

Make-Ahead Vegetable Salad

6 plum tomatoes, cut into eighths
1 green pepper, thinly sliced
1 red onion, thinly sliced
1 cucumber, peeled and thinly sliced
¾ cup cider vinegar
¼ cup water
2 tablespoons sugar
1½ teaspoons celery salt
1½ teaspoons mustard seed
¼ teaspoon salt
⅛ to ¼ teaspoon cayenne pepper
⅛ teaspoon pepper

Combine the tomatoes, green pepper, onion, and cucumber in a large bowl. Combine the remaining ingredients in a small saucepan. Bring to a boil, and boil for 1 minute. Pour over vegetables and toss to coat. Cover and refrigerate for 8 hours or overnight. Serve with a slotted spoon. Serves 8.

Curried Pineapple Rice

1 tablespoon olive oil

½ cup finely chopped onion

1 jalapeño pepper, seeded and chopped

2 garlic cloves, minced

1½ cups uncooked rice

1 tablespoon curry powder, or to taste

3 cups water or chicken broth

1 tablespoon soy sauce

1 20-ounce can unsweetened pineapple chunks, drained

1 pound fully cooked ham, cut into bite-sized pieces

In a medium saucepan, heat oil and sauté onion until tender. Stir in jalapeño, garlic, rice, and curry powder. Sauté until rice begins to brown. Add water or broth and soy sauce. Cover and bring to a boil. Reduce heat and simmer for 20 minutes, until liquid is all gone and rice is tender. Stir in pineapple chunks and ham. Serve at room temperature. Serves 8.

In the Same Place

One of the pleasures of friendship is having someone who is in the same place in life at the same time—someone who can understand everything you are going through. My friend Jan and I share this special bond.

Jan and I have been on the same track from the very beginning—we have the same exact birthdate—month, day, and year. When we discovered this fact, we began to make it a tradition to celebrate our birthdays together. On our thirtieth—when we were both single, successful career girls—we took a whirlwind trip through Europe together. We lived every fantasy—theater in London, the Orient Express, and Italy, where we enjoyed fending off the amorous Italian men. The trip culminated in dancing all night in Monte Carlo on our actual birthday.

Over the years, Jan and I stayed on similar tracks, now toward a more domestic life. We met the men of our dreams (both engineers and entrepreneurs), got engaged, and were married within two months of each other. By the time our thirty-fifth birthdays rolled around, we were again sharing an experience—we were both new mothers. We had quit our jobs to stay home with our babies and were feeling quite different from the wild girls we had been just five short years before.

To celebrate our birthdays, we decided to try to recapture some of our free spirit, and agreed to meet in San Francisco for dinner. As we waited for our table, we decided to go to the bar for

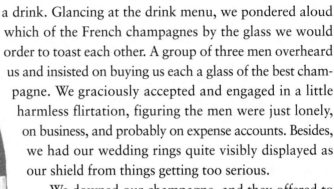

a drink. Glancing at the drink menu, we pondered aloud which of the French champagnes by the glass we would order to toast each other. A group of three men overheard us and insisted on buying us each a glass of the best champagne. We graciously accepted and engaged in a little harmless flirtation, figuring the men were just lonely, on business, and probably on expense accounts. Besides, we had our wedding rings quite visibly displayed as our shield from things getting too serious.

We downed our champagne, and they offered to buy us another. We demurely refused. But they kept insisting that we have another drink. "Just give me one good reason why you won't let us buy you another glass of champagne," one of them pushed.

Jan and I glanced at each other with a "what to do now?" kind of look.

Thinking quickly, she then blurted out, "If you really must know, it's because we're breastfeeding!"

That quickly ended any romantic ideas on their part, and any illusions on our part that we were the wild girls of our pasts.

—*Kathy Cordova*

Spiced Vinegar

Put a little of that spice back in your friendship with this little present. Be sure to remove the garlic and ginger after the first day, to prevent botulism.

1½ gallons cider vinegar

6 cloves garlic, halved

2 cups sugar

¼ cup whole cloves

¼ cup whole allspice

3 tablespoons celery seed

¼ cup mustard seed

5 tablespoons black peppercorns

¼ cup sliced fresh ginger

Combine all ingredients in a large saucepan. Heat on medium low until just before boiling. Remove from heat and transfer to a nonmetallic container with a tight lid. Steep for 24 hours. Remove garlic and ginger. Let vinegar steep for a month. Strain and pour into glass bottles. Cover tightly. Makes 1½ gallons.

> What is a friend? A single soul
> in two bodies.
>
> —ARISTOTLE

Blood Sisters

We peered through the broken glass in the garage window when we heard the screen door burst open and then slam against the side of the house. Granny was hollering out of the upstairs window, "Beth Ann, where are you going? Breakfast is almost ready. Beth Ann, you get in here this instant!"

Beth Ann's long, auburn pigtails flapped wildly against her shoulders as she ran toward us, extending her arm to reveal a tightly clenched fist. In an excited whisper she said, "I've got it! I've got it! But we have to be quick about it. If I don't get back upstairs soon, Granny is going to get the belt." She opened her palm to reveal a long hatpin with a large pearl attached to one end. "It's her favorite one. She uses it on Sundays to keep her hat on in church."

Cathy and I stared at the pin's pointy end. "I don't know," Cathy said, slowly shaking the blonde curls that surrounded her face like the petals of a sunflower. "It looks awfully big."

Beth Ann laughed. "What does that matter? We're only using the tip, silly."

I picked up the pin and gently ran my finger across the pointed end. "This will do the trick all right. Who wants to go first?"

Cathy took a step backward. "I don't know. Are you sure this is necessary?"

Beth Ann grabbed the pin. "Of course it is. We have to do this if we want to be blood brothers . . . or blood sisters or whatever you call it. It's part of the oath. Now we'd better hurry up or I'll get in trouble. Watch, I'll go first." With that she jabbed the tip of the pin into her thumb and then squeezed until a small red droplet appeared.

Cathy nervously bit her lip. "Did it hurt? Be honest or I'm not doing it." Beth Ann passed me the pin and said, "It only pinched for a minute. Now don't be a baby. Watch how Pam does it."

With one sharp sting, the hatpin pierced my flesh. I looked into Cathy's doubtful blue eyes and said, "See, that's all there is to it. Now hurry up before the blood starts to dry." Her hand trembled as she took the pin and tried three times. "I can't do it, you guys. It's going to hurt, I just know it."

Granny's head popped out of the upstairs window. "Beth Ann Smith, you get into this house right now. Your food is getting cold. What are you up to anyways?"

"Nothing Granny. I'm just talking to the girls. I'll be right up. I promise," she replied. Quickly, Beth Ann took the pin from Cathy and I grabbed Cathy's hand. Before she could pull away the pin was plunged into the tip of her thumb. "OUCH! I knew it would hurt. That's no fair, you guys."

I released her hand and said, "Don't be a whiner. Now squeeze out some blood."

We stood there silently while a delivery truck rattled and rumbled down the street, with the smell of bacon wafting through the broken pane that splashed sunlight across the spiderweb, making it sparkle like an ornament made of diamonds. Beth Ann took a deep breath and said, "Ready?"

Cathy and I inched closer to her and replied in unison, "Ready." With that, we pressed our blood-covered thumbs together and swore an oath of friendship that was even stronger than our devotion to Donny Osmond.

—*Pamela A. Rogers*

One's friends are that part of the human
race with which one can be human.

—GEORGE SANTAYANA

Ornamental Pleasures

It started fifteen years ago. Two weeks before Christmas, Kathleen gathered ten of her women friends together for a ladies' luncheon and tree-ornament swap. None of us knew each other, but we were all linked by our friendship with Kathleen. She's the kind of person who makes fun wherever she goes, and that lunch was no exception. We laughed, we traded stories of our lives. By the end, we vowed to do it again the following year.

And so it became a tradition. We don't see one another much in-between, but we look forward eagerly to our appointed lunch, and choose our ornaments with care. At some point along the way, Kathleen moved to Hawaii, but she always comes back to play hostess. It just wouldn't be Christmastime without it!

—S.S.

A friend is a present you give yourself.

—ROBERT LOUIS STEVENSON

Keepsake Ornaments

Want to give a friend a one-of-a-kind Christmas ornament? Consider these two easy ideas. You won't believe how great they look.

Cinnamon-Stick Bundle

> whole cinnamon sticks
> hot-glue gun
> plastic or silk holly sprig
> ribbon or raffia

Make a bundle of cinnamon sticks by gluing 5 or 6 together with the glue gun, one at a time, at their centers. Tie ribbon or raffia around center of bundle to conceal any hot-glue drops. Glue the holly sprig in the center of the ribbon. Tie a loop of ribbon or raffia at the center of ornament for a hanger. Makes 1.

Miniature Vine Wreaths

tiny vine wreaths (available at craft stores)
dried flowers and herbs, such as lavender, artemisia, globe amaranth,
strawflowers, pearly everlasting
hot-glue gun
thin ribbon for hanger

Hot-glue flowers in a pleasing arrangement. Tie on ribbon hanger at top of wreath. You may want to hot-glue a flower on the ribbon where it meets the wreath. Makes 1.

Mustang Tuesdays

At four o'clock every Tuesday afternoon, John and I would drive from the Queens campus of St. John's University to the Arthur Kill Correctional Facility, where we taught inmates in the university's external degree program. John had been teaching Public Speaking at St. John's for twenty years before I returned to my alma mater as Assistant Dean. We quickly became a team—arguing for academic integrity at the Faculty Council, organizing poetry readings, spending much free time 'round the Speech Department's coffeepot fomenting revolution against the university's medieval president, or inviting colleagues to deliver the lecture they would like to be remembered for.

John's just-off-campus apartment was a clubhouse for students, alumni, faculty, and even a few eccentric administrators like me. The pad's unkempt nature fit perfectly with its drop-in informality. John was obsessive about keeping a clean toilet, but his dedication to housekeeping did not extend beyond that tiled space. If I or any of John's other pals complained about the dishes in the sink, or the cobwebs and dust, or the holes in the screen door, we'd be directed to the relevant chemicals and housewares. John's apartment . . . was ours. How else would John have found time to teach his classes, write his articles, prepare his own distinguished lectures, and moderate the discussions that ran through the nights until the wine bottles lay uncorked and dry?

When I established the prison program, I recruited John to teach, and scheduled his class on the same evening as my own Creative Writing class. After each Tuesday's Curriculum Committee meeting, we'd leave campus in my Mustang and follow the Belt Parkway along New York Bay to the Verrazano Narrows Bridge, clear to the west end of Staten Island.

And, in contrast to all the talk at meetings and at John's house, we'd say not a word to each other. We didn't feel compelled to entertain each other or keep conversation going. Silence was not the rule, but our habit on these Tuesday trips—a pleasure that could never be replaced by a drive by oneself. We simply enjoyed each other's presence.

—James Penha

Some of the most rewarding and
beautiful moments of a friendship happen
in the unforeseen open spaces between
planned activities. It is important that you
allow these spaces to exist.

—Christine Leefeldt

Some Things Never Change

Deb and I met in a college poetry class, and we've been friends ever since. In the years that have followed, she's been my study partner, my roommate, my guinea pig for new recipes, my shoulder to cry on, my traveling companion, and my maid of honor. Though we now live hundreds of miles apart, we're still the best of friends. I've got the phone bills to prove it. And when we do get to spend time together, it's as though we're still two college kids, sharing an apartment on campus.

Over the holidays, I spent a week back home. Deb's birthday was that week, so the two of us planned to go out for dinner to celebrate. We decided to go to an Indian restaurant—because we still haven't been able to find anyone else who shares our love of Indian food.

As we ate, we chatted as if we'd been apart for three days instead of three months. We talked about work and the books we were reading and the movies we wanted to see. We laughed about the good old days and predicted our futures as we ate from each other's plates.

After dinner, we drove back to Deb's apartment for dessert— to recreate her twenty-first birthday. That year, her birthday was the day before a big final exam, so going out to celebrate in style wasn't really a wise choice. Instead, we took a study break in our apartment. Now, several years later, we celebrated the same way—

by making a big batch of chocolate frosting and eating it straight out of the pan. We passed the pan back and forth, watching reruns of *The Muppet Show* just as we had done years ago.

I'm confident that, for Deb and me, some things will never change. We may move to different states—or even different countries. We may change jobs and start families. But no matter where we live or what happens in our lives, we'll also be there for each other. Years from now, we'll still be able to share our stories and laugh together. We'll still spend hours discussing our favorite books. We'll still love John Cusack movies and *The Muppet Show*.

And we'll still celebrate her birthday by eating chocolate frosting right out of the pan.

—*Kristin Dreyer Kramer*

> Wherever you are it is your friends that
> make your world.
>
> —William James

Fabulous Fudge

Sometimes all the two of you need is a little chocolate. This is my grandmother's recipe for no-fail fudge. It's a great friend-ship sweetener.

1 7-ounce jar Marshmallow Fluff

²/₃ cup evaporated milk

1¹/₃ cups sugar

¹/₄ cup butter

¹/₄ teaspoon salt

1 12-ounce package semisweet chocolate chips

1 teaspoon vanilla

Combine all ingredients except chocolate and vanilla in a medium saucepan. Bring to a boil. Boil, stirring constantly, for 5 minutes. Remove from heat, add chocolate chips, stirring, until all chocolate has melted. Add vanilla and stir. Turn into 8-inch-square buttered pan. Let cool until hardened. Cut into squares. Makes 2½ pounds.

The Laughing Fit

The two of us were at a meditation retreat for a week. A silent retreat. Luckily, we knew ourselves well enough to know that we couldn't resist talking. So we had arranged to share a room, and we perfected the art of whispering in our beds each evening like a couple of schoolgirls. Toward the end of the week, as we lay there, one of us said something funny to the other. I don't remember who or what. And we started to laugh. And laugh. Quickly we clutched our pillows to our faces, desperately trying not to be heard. Tears rolled down our cheeks as we tried to control ourselves. When one of us began to gain some modicum of composure, she'd look at the other and burst out again. It went on and on—ten minutes at least. My sides ached from laughing and the effort to restrain myself. Part of me was more joyful than I have been in my whole life. The other part was worrying about getting in trouble for breaking silence. When we finally calmed down (the only thing that worked was ignoring one another), I realized I hadn't laughed that hard in forty years. What fun!

—*M. J. Ryan*

The average person living to age 70 has
613,000 hours of life. This is too long
a period not to have fun.

—ANONYMOUS

Divine Rights

The year was 1964 and I was a teenager. The Pope was not only coming to New York but was scheduled to pass under the windows of our classrooms on Madison Avenue in Manhattan. We were given strict instructions to return to class promptly after lunch, and not to join the swelling crowds of people. More precisely, we were not permitted to be late or cut class to see the motorcade.

Alas, the draw was too great. My friend and I opted to risk the consequences in order to see the Pope. Satisfied but afraid, we returned to class thirty-five minutes late, to be met by the ominous glare of our teacher. Her arm extended, and finger pointing to the door, she commanded, "To the principal's office!"

The principal, Mrs. Sadie Brown, a wizened old woman in her nineties, listened quietly as we told of our indiscretion. She said nothing. Then, reaching to her desk, she scribbled something on a piece of paper. She folded the paper, speaking only to instruct us to hand it to our teacher. Safely out of view, my friend and I opened the paper. It read, simply: "Papal dispensation."

—*Pat Gallant*

If you obey all of the rules, you miss
all of the fun.

—KATHERINE HEPBURN

A Cup of Tea

It was a simple moment—one I anticipated after a taxing morning. Promptly at two o'clock I heard the car door slam and conjured up the smell of scones and tea biscuits even before the back door opened. Lisa was bringing afternoon tea!

She greeted me with a booming laugh and a brimming basket. Starched linen napkins, an English teapot and cozy, Battenberg lace runner, and Delft cups met my gaze. My nose caught the whiff of freshly baked goodies hidden from sight; what tea would accompany them today? Earl Grey or English breakfast tea? Maybe I would splurge with something bolder, like an Indian or Kenyan tea.

Enjoying the ritual we loved so well, Lisa and I traded initial pleasantries as we laid the table. The lace runner alighted on the table like a butterfly seeking rest. I placed the teapot and cups in their accustomed positions, while Lisa apportioned the delicacies on china plates. Within minutes the interchange drifted towards the second level of conversation—personal concerns and reports of family matters.

Sipping and tasting, we plunged into the sea of conversation. The ebb and flow eventually deposited us on the sand of scone crumbs, in the shadow of a tea cozy. Reluctantly we folded napkins and repacked the familiar basket as the clock chimed three times. Another tea time was closing, and yet this one was unlike all the others: Lisa was moving to Africa where her family would work in an orphanage.

We hesitated to voice our thoughts, simultaneously clutching the basket as each one reached for an errant corner of the lace runner. Wordlessly, our eyes and hearts whispered, "Until next time."

Unhurriedly, she gathered the items and turned to leave. I watched as the door opened and closed. Glancing back to the table, I noticed that Lisa had forgotten one of her cups. I started to knock on the kitchen window to get her attention, but immediately realized the cup was actually not forgotten. Instead, I held a keepsake of a simple pleasure of friendship—a shared moment.

—*Diane H. Pitts*

> Find yourself a cup of tea; the teapot
> is behind you. Now tell me about
> hundreds of things.
>
> —SAKI

An Afternoon Tea Party

Here are some sandwiches served at a traditional tea. Don't forget to cut the crust off the bread.

Watercress Sandwiches

1 bunch watercress
8 tablespoons butter
4 teaspoons lemon juice
8 slices white bread
salt to taste

Wash watercress and trim leaves off stems. Set aside. Mix the butter and lemon juice in a food processor or blender. Spread butter lightly on bread. Arrange watercress leaves on butter. Salt lightly. Top with bread slice. Cut into 4 pieces. Makes 16 tea-sized sandwiches.

Cucumber Sandwiches

1 large cucumber
salt to taste
mayonnaise to taste
butter to taste
4 slices bread

Remove seeds and slice cucumber as thinly as possible. Place in pan and sprinkle with salt. Cover with paper towels to absorb moisture and let sit for 1 hour.

Spread mayonnaise and butter on bread. Arrange cucumbers attractively on top. Cut into quarters. Makes 16 open-faced tea-sized sandwiches.

Strawberry Sandwiches

2 tablespoons butter

$^1/_2$ cup confectioners' sugar

2 teaspoons lemon juice

4 large strawberries

8 slices bread

Combine all ingredients except bread in food processor. Allow to harden in refrigerator for 3 hours. Spread on bread and cut each slice into 4. Makes 24 open-faced tea-sized sandwiches.

Poppy Seed Scones

Here's a simple recipe for the next tea party you throw. Scones are also great at breakfast time. If you want to be truly British, try serving them with lemon curd.

$^1/_4$ cup sugar

2 cups all-purpose flour

1 tablespoon poppy seeds

1 tablespoon baking powder

$^1/_4$ teaspoon salt

$^1/_3$ cup butter

2 tablespoons lemon juice in $^3/_4$ cup milk

Preheat oven to 425° F. In a large bowl, combine sugar, flour, poppy seeds, baking powder, and salt. Cut in butter until mixture is crumbly. Add milk mixture until blended. Turn onto a floured board and knead six times. Shape into a ball, then form into an 8-inch circle. Cut into 8 pieces, as if cutting a pizza. Place on a greased cookie sheet and bake for 12–15 minutes, or until scones are lightly browned. Makes 8 scones.

There are few hours in life more
agreeable than the hour dedicated to the
ceremony known as afternoon tea.

—HENRY JAMES

The Perfect Cup of Tea

There are over 2,000 teas in the world, but they all come from one plant—the tropical Camellia Sinensis, a relative of the common garden camellia. The variations in taste are created in the method of processing, which results in four main groups—black, oolong, green, and white. Black tea accounts for over 90 percent of the tea consumption in the Western world. And when it comes to black tea, no one does it better than the British. They raised tea drinking to the status of a meal—a late afternoon affair complete with small sandwiches, cakes, and other treats to tide you over until dinner.

If you want to host a tea for friends, make sure that the tea itself is brewed properly. No steeping in your cup allowed—you *must* have a teapot and, preferably, a tea cozy to keep the pot warm.

Directions: Fill kettle with cold water and bring to a hard boil. Scald teapot with boiling water. Place 1 teabag per cup in the teapot, or, for true authenticity, 1 rounded teaspoon of loose tea per cup into an infuser in the pot. Let steep for 3 minutes. Remove infuser and serve. Ah!

COMFORT AND CARING

Friendship is born at that moment when one person
says to another: What! You too? I thought
I was the only one.

—C. S. LEWIS

What are your thoughts about whether I should let Brittany get her belly button pierced? How do I deal with this dead-end job? Help—I feel fat and ugly and unloved! Friends are the folks who are there for us in good times and bad, offering advice as well as the warmth of their caring. Being able to count on that support is one of friendship's greatest satisfactions.

Wonder Women

The briefcase I carry every day to my university job holds the usual things—books, folders, calendar, keys, lunch, and oh yes, a tiny yellow-haired doll with a short skirt, a cape, and an attitude.

Four years ago, when I decided to move from Texas to Illinois for graduate school, I considered all the important issues—the curriculum, the professors, scholarships, future careers. I never thought about the possibility of friends. So imagine my delight when, in my first year, a small group of female students started to meet about once a week for lunch. On the surface we had little in common. We hailed from different hometowns and economic circumstances. Some were married, some single. Recent college graduates mixed with some midlife career changers. Even within the same graduate program we had chosen different areas of specialization.

"Ladies who lunch," someone once called us. That made us laugh. We were far more likely to eat BLTs in a basement cafeteria than to leisurely sip Chardonnay at a five-star restaurant. Conversation ranged from movies and nail polish to more serious issues of health, relationships, and finances. It was like a good ol' girls club, except that it wasn't exclusive. We regularly invited others to join us, like the homesick blonde from South Africa and the motorcycle-riding ex-lawyer. Somehow we ended up calling ourselves "sisters," and the name stuck.

Two years later, with graduation nearing, the archivist in the group brought a package of small, plastic female superheroes to lunch and handed them out to the five of us. Cheap plastic figures about two inches tall, they were painted with the kind of out-of-bounds coloring that would likely get you written up in kindergarten.

When the group reunited at a conference two years ago, someone mentioned the dolls at dinner. One by one, the dolls peeked from briefcases and purses. Amazingly, we had all kept them close by as we made our way into the world, a small reminder of a time when any dream was possible with the support of your friends.

—*Michelle Mach*

Alone we can do so little;
together we can do so much.

—HELEN KELLER

Friendship Blooms

I jog, my mind racing. Soon I break into a run. I need to get away. From the rut of office, the disease at home, colleagues at elbow, boss with a hammer. I plough through my day, each day. Cancer greets me at home every night, my bedside table lined with boxes of medicine and packets of syringes. My wife lies in bed, head shorn of her raven curls, telling me of the aches that filled her day. I change, feed us both, sleep, and get up the next morning to lead another such day.

But today, as I jog, my legs fail, my spirits sag. I peer through the misted haze, and see only grey. I shiver.

Just then—specks of red, white, orange, and purple catch my eye. I run toward them. I reach a woman. Almost hidden behind her are baskets overflowing with garlands and rose petals: gladioli in red, white, and purple; long-stemmed tuberoses; yellow and orange marigolds. She sits surrounded by their scented glory. A smile curves up to light her wrinkled face as I near.

A few fragrant breaths later, I drive home, her cheery chatter pealing in my ears, happiness spilling from the corners of my mustache, and a yellow marigold garland draped over my left arm. As I hang it by my wife's bedside, her chapped lips break into a smile.

Next morning I stop by my flower lady. "Thank you. Your garland cheered my sick wife." Her eyes ask more. I kneel by her and pour out my story.

She shakes her head. "My flowers know they wither tomorrow, yet they bloom with such happiness and abandon. Laugh you must."

I go home with a rose garland this time.

I now wait for the sun to rise. I enjoy my jog. But what I like most is to sit next to her flowers and chat. Things seem bright around her. She has two daughters, I now know. Lovely they are, but too busy to worry over their mom. I tell her about my daughter who never had a chance, dying at birth.

We share a few moments, sometimes a cup of tea. I buy a garland and leave. Two months pass this way, my wife deteriorates, then leaves me, for God.

I can't jog anymore. I seek my flower lady out and drop down with a thump. She understands. She just holds my hand and sits.

As I get up to leave, she pushes an orange garland into my arms.

"For whom?" I stammer, and stare at her.

"For you," she says. "You breathe it. When you find a new love, you share with her."

She stops my hand as I fish a wallet out of my pocket. "You're my friend. Not a customer."

I turn and wrap my arms around her sunken shoulders. I wet her shawl with my tears. "See you tomorrow, friend." I call out and walk away, burying my nose in the orange blossoms.

—*Swapna Goel*

A friend is one to whom one may pour out all the contents of one's heart, chaff and grain together, knowing that the gentlest of hands will take and sift it, keep what is worth keeping and with a breath of kindness blow the rest away.

—ARABIAN PROVERB

Heartfelt Wreath

Sending messages of affection expressed through the language of flowers is a tradition that has thrived since the Victorian age. You can use any dried flowers you want, but if you follow the suggestions here and use pansies, you are saying, "You occupy my thoughts."

foam heart base (available at craft stores) or buy a piece of foam and cut out a heart yourself

green potpourri, enough to cover heart

dried flowers, including pansies

dried fern

craft glue

hot-glue gun

Cover the top and sides of the heart with craft glue, and press the potpourri in to cover completely. Allow to dry thoroughly, then arrange flowers and fern in a pleasing arrangement and hot-glue them in place.

A Friend in Deed

I remember it like it was yesterday, although I haven't seen or spoken to Alex in close to fifteen years. I was dying. I was lying on the floor of my overpriced Seattle apartment, staring into the orange shag carpet that filled the room. I had spent most of my cash on a waterbed, waiting for my girlfriend to arrive from Ann Arbor. She never did. My last $40 went for a pair of blue polyester pants so that I could take a job waiting tables in a restaurant that boasted 150 different kinds of beer, an owner with a Welsh accent, and an Irish cook with a passion for strippers.

I had been working there for one week when the tickle in my throat started. I used all of my tips (and there weren't many of them) to go to the clinic for a checkup. The verdict: strep throat. I was not allowed near people, food, or drink. Period. My new boss, for whom I had spent my last $40 on the ugliest pants I could have imagined, fired me over the phone, and there I was, three days later, curled up on the floor. I had no money for medicine. I had no money for food. I had a large, empty waterbed staring me in the face that I couldn't bear to use, and the only comfort I could find was that the teal blue appliances, the poorly stained cabinets, and the orange shag rug were quite possibly the last things I would see in my life—I found that hysterical.

The knock on my door surprised me into wakefulness. It could only be the landlord, wondering why my slick-talking entrepreneurial self was late with the rent. But it was my friend Alex. Alejandro Sosa, tagged with the name of a drug dealer from an Al Pacino movie and fresh from a car ride from Portland. He was bored. He thought he'd look me up.

The happiness on his face disappeared after one look at me. He dragged me to my feet, hauled me down to his car, took me to the doctor, bought my medicine and a big dinner of teriyaki chicken to go, and dropped me back on the shag rug an hour later.

We barely said ten words during the whole visit. Later that night he climbed back into his car and drove to Portland. I stared at the medicine bottle, now standing on the shag carpet in front of me, and I smiled. "That jerk," I thought, and coughed into my hand. I'd always hated surprises.

—*Mark Kaplan*

True friendship comes when silence
between two people is comfortable.

—ANONYMOUS

Sickbed Surprises

Got a sick friend? How about buying a pretty basket or one of those lovely gift bags and filling it with inexpensive items—a candle, some lotion, an ice pack? Place it outside the front door, ring the doorbell, and run away. Or try a surprising variation on that traditional sickbed favorite—flowers. Buy a small wooden box, make a bed of dried moss (available at craft stores), then add a few buds of fresh flowers on top (use florist water tubes to keep flowers fresh). A great surprise when opened!

Every gift from a friend is a wish
for your happiness.

—RICHARD BACH

The Price of Friendship

School was out for the day, and I dug through my backpack to find my bus pass in my wallet. But after about two minutes, I still hadn't found my little black wallet. Suddenly I realized that I had left it on my dresser that morning.

"Oh damn," I breathed, leaning back with my eyes closed. "What am I supposed to do?" I dug through my pack one more time, and found a spare dollar bill. My heart lifted at the sight, but dropped again as I remembered that it took a dollar and ten cents to get on the bus. I got up and walked to the bus stop with a heavy heart.

When I reached the stop, my problem evaporated as friends started talking to me. It was the usual—who likes whom now, who broke up, who did what embarrassing thing today. . . . I was talking happily until someone shouted, "206 bus!" My bus. I groaned as I remembered my dilemma. A boy standing by heard my groan and asked, "What's wrong?"

"Oh, I forgot my bus pass and I'm a dime short," I replied.

"I'll give you ten cents out of my quarter," he offered. "That'll take care of both of our fares."

I looked up. This boy whom I didn't know well, whom I had only talked to a few times and had a few classes with, would give me a dime?

He gestured, smiling. "Come on, the bus won't wait." I returned his smile with a grin, and picked up my things. A glow surrounded him as he stood in front of me: the glow of a friend for the price of a dime.

—*Tammy Lee*

Depth of friendship does not depend on
length of acquaintance.

—Sir Rabindranath Tagore

Meant to Be

I've known my friend Jessa for seven years. We're in daily contact, and she knows all the secrets of my life: my shoplifting at eight, how I cheated on my ex, and how I'm terrified to become a mother. I know about her bee phobia, her college bout with anorexia, and the way she met her husband (through *Match.com*, but they tell people it was a blind date).

We were destined to connect—two different mutual friends tried to introduce us. The first time we were at a birthday party. "You and Jessa have so much in common," the host said. "Both writers, both ex-marketers for computer companies." We exchanged business cards, but nothing came of it. Several years later, another friend attempted to hook us up.

The coincidence seemed meaningful, so I pulled out her old business card and e-mailed her, noting both friends we had in common, and how certain they were that our paths needed to cross. A friendship was struck immediately, and this time we stayed in touch. We e-mail each other about movies we've seen, houseguests who annoy, restaurants to die for, books we love, and struggles in our relationships.

Yet here's the thing: we've only met in person three times. I moved away right after we made contact. We met live for the second time when I was back in town once over the holidays and we had coffee. The third time was her wedding a few years ago. When I went to greet her at the reception, it was a little awkward— someone I knew so intimately, yet had only seen twice in three years. I don't even own a picture of her.

But even though we have no history of going to school together or being coworkers, and even lacking a legacy of phone conversations, our connection is deep. I check my e-mail each day for an update on how her deck is coming, or if there was a line across the wand on the pregnancy test. My house-hunting trials seem less overwhelming with the knowledge that I can log on and vent to my friend, and that a sympathetic response will come quickly in return.

Maybe it's about being able to put my thoughts together ahead of time, more like old-fashioned letter writing than the continual interruptions of cell phones and waiters in our daily personal interaction. Or knowing I can fully express my thoughts and feelings and that the friend on the other end will take the time to truly listen and respond in kind. Whatever our friendship is based on—dropping out of high tech to become writers, being childless and the same age, working from home, or simply a love of letter writing—I'm grateful for the comfort and reassurance offered by these messages from my e-mail friend.

—Jaime Johnson

No distance of place or lapse of time
can lessen the friendship of those who
are thoroughly persuaded of
each other's worth.

—ROBERT SOUTHEY

Homemade Soap

Send an e-mail friend a gift of soap to let her know you're thinking of her. It's so easy. Just make sure you start with meltable soap, which is available at craft stores. I used an angel cookie cutter, and then sent them to friends to thank them for being angels in my life.

> meltable soap
> few drops of your favorite essential oil
> few drops food coloring of your choice
> cookie cutters

Cut the soap into 1-inch pieces. Place in glass, microwaveable bowl and microwave according to soap package directions. Add essential oil and stir. Add food coloring until you have the color you want. Pour melted soap into a foil pan and set aside to harden. Press into desired shapes with cookie cutters by applying firm but gentle pressure.

Even Easier Gift Soap

Don't feel like making soap? Buy a few beautiful bars and wrap them up creatively to give them a personal touch. Here are some ideas:

- Buy muslin bags at a craft store, and tie with silk ribbon.
- Cut up a brown paper bag to use as wrapping paper, and tie with raffia for a rustic look.
- Buy a loofah sponge and a large bow. Place soap on top of sponge and tie with bow.
- Find a small wooden box and use it as a container.
- Buy an attractive soap dish and attach a cake of soap with a silk cord.

Everything Was Just Fine

It began as such a simple thing, only a bit inconvenient. I live in San Miguel de Allende, Mexico, a beautiful Spanish Colonial town in the heart of the Sierra Madres. It's a town of artists, writers, and theatrical types—most of whom, like me, were originally from the U.S. and Canada.

Living in Mexico affords a comfortable lifestyle, with a few generally minor inconveniences: Medicaid does not cover hospitalization, and San Miguel has no top-level hospital of its own. Therefore, hospitalization must be paid for, and participating hospitals are at a distance.

One day, I went for a checkup in San Luis Potosí, driving the 120 miles north at a comfortable pace, expecting to return the same afternoon. However, the doctor's exam took longer than the drive, extending late into the afternoon and ending with the decision that surgery was required immediately.

My family was in the U.S., and I'd made no provision for my house and dog to be cared for, since I hadn't planned an extended absence. I immediately called Russ. He had keys to my home, loved my dog, and had knowledge of all the workings of my house. I'd bought it from him. I was concerned enough about the surgery that worries about my homestead were the last thing I needed.

The surgery went well and, three days later, Russ took the bus from San Miguel to San Luis to drive me home. The doctors had refused to release me alone. When Russ arrived the morning of my release, he appeared somewhat worn, albeit as cheerful and uplifting as usual. "Everything was just fine at the house," he told me.

Days later I learned that he'd experienced a series of minor catastrophes while watching my house: a broken water main, phone disconnection due to nonpayment of bill (an error on the phone company's part), lost keys, and so forth. He never mentioned them. A final trial had awaited him when he checked the bus schedules. The minimum time he could make the trip, a three-bus connection, was six hours. And that required that he leave San Miguel at three a.m. He'd been traveling nearly all night before taxiing to the hospital to escort me out.

I never told him that I learned of all he'd gone through for my sake. But I threw him one heck of a birthday party when the time came.

—*Allen McGill*

When true friends meet in adverse hour,

'Tis like a sunbeam through a shower.

A watery way an instant seen,

The darkly closing clouds between.

—SIR WALTER SCOTT

Thank-You Thrills

Have a friend who's helped you through some difficulty? Surprise him or her with a thank-you present: Create a surprise party, send flowers out of the blue, or drop a $100 bill and a note in her purse when she's not looking. Or write a letter of heartfelt thanks and deliver it with a basket of his favorite cookies. It doesn't have to be expensive or complicated. However you choose to honor his or her friendship, you both will get a kick out of the surprise—you from thinking of it, and your friend from receiving it.

Smiling Faces

I have a photo on my office desk. When life gets particularly challenging—my boss doesn't appreciate my efforts, I have to work late again, I'm feeling lonely—I look at it. It is a goofy picture of me and my four best friends at the beach years ago. It reminds me of the fun we had together, and the fact that they are still there for me. We may live far apart now, but almost weekly, I get a call from one of them checking in, or a joke or inspirational quote via e-mail. When I was going through my divorce, they took turns visiting and spent hours on the phone listening to me vent. Just looking at the photo of their smiling faces makes me smile, no matter what is going on in my life.

—Alicia Alvres

A life without a friend is
a life without sun.

—GERMAN PROVERB

Hike to Happiness

In this hectic world, my friend Marieke and I sometimes have trouble finding time to eat and sleep. By the end of the week, we feel exhausted and stressed. But, on most Sunday mornings, we pause from the daily grind to get together, find a trail, and start walking. Our paths may have started from different corners of the world—Marieke is from Holland via South Africa, and I'm from rural upstate New York—but we both love to explore our Sonoran Desert home. We each consider ourselves lucky to have found a friend who enjoys hiking.

In a couple of hours, we cover a lot of territory. First, it's catch-up time—what's new in our lives, or our children's lives. Somewhere along the way, Marieke teaches me Dutch, and I teach her geology. Books are reviewed, business decisions made, local politics discussed, and solutions to the world's problems devised. We use each other as a sounding board for new ideas and as an outlet for frustrations built up through the week. There's something about nature, and exercise, and a sympathetic companion that makes seemingly insurmountable problems shrink back to realistic proportions.

We make many discoveries on our hikes, both simple and profound: windmills and bears, flowers and crystals, awesome vistas and hidden spaces. Because we don't like to return the way we came, we often blaze our own trail, and gather a few cuts and scratches along the way. That's true with our lives, too, I suppose. In the last ten or twelve years, we've survived career changes, medical problems, and children growing up and out.

Most mornings, we end up in Marieke's kitchen for a cup of coffee with her husband. Then, just to keep our brains as limber as our bodies, we solve the Sunday morning puzzle from the public broadcast radio station, or unscramble the jumble in the Sunday paper. By late morning, family obligations and unfinished chores begin to gnaw at the edges of our consciousness, and we part to tackle life again. But our batteries have been recharged and our spirits lifted. Sunday's simple pleasures have restored our balance once again.

—Bonnie Kline

Life's truest happiness is found in
friendships we make along the way.

—ANONYMOUS

Giant Popovers

Invite a friend to brunch on a lazy Sunday morning and give these popovers a try. A real treat that is the height of simplicity. Great with butter and jam or honey.

6 eggs
¼ cup peanut or canola oil
2 cups milk
1¾ cups unsifted flour
1½ teaspoons salt

Preheat oven to 375° F. In large bowl, combine eggs and oil. Beat in milk, flour, and salt. Pour batter into 10 well-oiled custard cups. Place custard cups on baking sheet. Bake 1 hour, or until firm and brown. Makes 10 large popovers.

Surrogate Friend

December 24 arrived with heavy snow that clung stubbornly to the roads. Highways closed and the authorities issued travel advisories.

"Let it snow," I thought. It was my first Christmas Eve without my mother, and the sadness of that thought battered the day's excitement. Any excuse not to leave the shelter of my small apartment was good.

The telephone rang. I ignored it and went to my bedroom to bury my face in the softness of my pillow, hoping to muffle the demanding trill. It was eight o'clock, and I was supposed to be at my friend Rebecca's house for dinner. "I'm doing her a favor by not being there," I thought. "How could I be joyful when I felt so lousy? I want to be left alone." My eyes fluttered with the weight of the tears that would not stop. My heart felt as heavy as the falling snow; my grief piled high. *How do I stop missing my mother?*

I must have drifted off to sleep, for I awoke with a start. Someone pounded at the front door. I tiptoed to the window and looked through the frosted pane. Seeing Rebecca's car parked out front, I padded back to bed and drew the covers over my head.

"Girlfriend," she shouted. "I know you're in there! Answer the door!"

"Leave me alone!" I shouted back.

The floorboards creaked in the hallway. I heard paper rustling as she slid something under the door. "Merry Christmas," she called out.

Not answering the door made me feel worse, if that was possible. She was my best friend. Since grade school, we were inseparable. Most people mistook us for sisters. Her father and sister died in a car accident when she was eight years old. As a result, her mother had to return to work, and Rebecca was pretty much left to fend for herself. We had always been there for each other, but this time, I didn't want her or anyone else near me.

When I was sure she had left, I retrieved the small, flat package wrapped simply in gold foil. Carrying it to the bench by the window, I sat down and unwrapped it. It was a gold pen and a blank journal. When I opened the front cover, a bookmark fell out, and on it a note:

Dear Sister Friend: My words won't heal the pain. But your own words can. Love, Rebecca

I stared at the blank pages. A single tear fell, and the paper absorbed it. I wrote my name on the first page and looked at it for a long time.

Over the following months, my grief took refuge within the pages of the book. Tears fell on to the paper as often as words. Prayers tearfully written, faith renewed. As my heart healed, so did my understanding of the friendship Rebecca and I shared. Even though I pushed her away at a difficult time, she found a way to help me communicate my grief, by giving me this "surrogate" friend.

One night, I picked up the phone and dialed her number. She answered on the second ring. "Looks like the snow is melting," I said. Spring was just around the corner.

—S. A. *(Shae) Cooke*

One of the most beautiful qualities of
true friendship is to understand
and to be understood.

—SENECA

One-of-a-Kind Memory Book

This is so easy to make, even someone who is all thumbs can manage it. You can give this to a friend, to use to record dreams, to list books she's read, or to use as a daily journal.

thin wrapping paper, in two coordinating colors or patterns, one for outside cover, one for inside

blank book

aerosol adhesive

ribbon or raffia

Pick one piece of wrapping paper for the cover. Open the book and place it face-up on the paper. Cut the paper 1 inch larger than the opened book on all sides. Remove the book. Place the paper face-down on your work surface. Spray the back of the paper with adhesive.

Place the spine of the book in the dead center of the paper; press gently. Working slowly from the spine to the edge of the front cover, to avoid wrinkles, smooth one side of the paper over the front cover of the book, pressing out any bubbles as you go toward the edge. Rub the paper into the groove along the spine with a pencil end. Repeat for the back of the book.

As if you were wrapping a present, fold excess paper from sides, top, and bottom of the front and back covers to the inside of the book. Press and smooth paper.

Cut ribbon or raffia long enough to serve as a marker (at least 1 inch longer than book height). Place the top of the ribbon or raffia inside the top of the spine. Cut notches in the paper along the top and bottom of the book at the spine, and fold excess paper in at the spine, securing the ribbon or raffia as you fold in.

Cut the second paper into two sheets, each ¼-inch smaller than the inside of the book covers on all sides. Turn over and spray with adhesive. Press the sheets to the inside of the front and back covers, to cover over the excess paper from the outside cover.

The Birthday Call

When my phone rang at nine-thirty in the morning on December 25th, I knew it was Jane even before I looked at the glowing caller identification screen. She always remembers my birthday. My parents, who are perpetually afraid of waking me up, never call before ten, and most of my other friends—even the ones who, like me, are Jewish—were still asleep on that rare day off.

For three-and-a-half years, Jane and I worked together for the state government in Massachusetts. We sat and chatted many times each day, making the short journey over three grey cubicles and down one row, to talk about the traffic, a TV show, or undeserved criticism that one of us had received from a well-to-do colleague with a vast collection of hideous, fluorescent shoes.

When an accident left me carless, I became Jane's regular morning traffic copilot, her wacky sidekick on a private talk show that no one but the two of us could hear or see. We grew closer quickly, and decided that we were surrogate siblings shortly after learning that we shared a unique bond: we were both Jews born during the Christmas holiday, eighteen years and one day apart. After a lifetime of friends handing us belated birthday cards in mid-January (or, understandably, forgetting completely), Jane and I were both thrilled to have a new partner-in-time.

When I moved from Boston to New York City, our morning chats in Jane's maroon Toyota—now evoked by a Matchbox replica of her car on my new desk—became biweekly e-mails and occasional phone calls. Still, we both know that there are two days each year when we can count on each other to resurrect our consecutive conversations, two days when much of the country is off reveling in another special birthday and the love of family and friends, two days when we get to share in the joy of celebrating each other.

I called Jane on the 24th, while she was getting dressed to go to dinner at a restaurant that she had carefully chosen for the occasion. We exchanged tales of crazy family members, caught up on stories about former colleagues, and discussed whether she should leave the Toyota at home and splurge on a cab ride in order to properly enjoy an extra glass of wine with dinner.

When the phone rang on the 25th, I knew she would sing "Happy Birthday" and fill me in on all the details about her evening—the restaurant, the dinner, her friends, the wine (she splurged!)—and then ask me about my plans for the day, my partner, my family.

"Hi, honey," she said, finishing her song. "Did I wake you up?"

"No," I beamed, alert but still snuggled under piles of covers. I'd been waiting for her call all year.

—Eric Pliner

A friendship can weather most things and
thrive in thin soil—but it needs a little
mulch of letters and phone calls and
small silly presents every so often—just to
save it from drying out completely.

—PAM BROWN

Real Gift Wrap

Next time you want to give a friend a bottle of wine, olive oil,
or vinegar, consider wrapping it in a lovely dishtowel that she
can keep. It's easy. Open the towel and lay the bottle horizon-
tally on it, with the bottom about 2 inches from the edge. Roll
the bottle up, and tie it every two inches with ribbon. Fold bottom edges in and tape with double-sided sticky tape. Cinch the
top with more ribbon tied into a beautiful bow.

Lightening the Load

Dear Sis,
How are you pulling the wagons of life that side? Back to me,
my load is a heavy burden . . . .

I put down Zodwa's letter and smile. Her introduction is our shared joke of the clichéd beginnings that Zimbabwean students use to start their letters. As a high-school English teacher in rural Zimbabwe for two years, I graded too many letters that began the same way. Zodwa lived two houses from me. She worked at the local clinic, and in the evenings and on weekends, we would amble over to each other's houses. She would scold me to wear shoes so the thorns on the dirt path wouldn't imbed themselves in my feet. I would tell her she wasn't my mother. She'd laugh and retort, "No, I'm the younger, wiser sister."

Sisters? We couldn't be more different. She's Zimbabwean; I'm American. She's as black as the night sky, while I am so white, she once told me, that I glow in the dark. We cemented our friendship over Crazy Eights and long strolls. We began calling each other Sis, an endearment among Zimbabwean woman.

As I sit with her letter, I realize it's been five years since I last hugged her or watched her eyes crinkle at the corners. In some ways I am amazed that we have continued writing to each other for so long. Zodwa struggles to keep her family clothed, schooled, and fed in a country with such economic hardship and social strife that a loaf of bread is something people can only afford once a month. I am amazed that the mail even reaches Zodwa, that it's not discarded by disgusted postal employees opening letters to hunt for American dollars.

The last five years have also brought changes for me that could have disrupted the flow of mail and our friendship. I have moved twice, and my days are full with the communications of a computerized society. Still, I find time to write to Zodwa.

Or rather, I make the time to write. And that perhaps is why I am not so amazed that we have continued writing over the years and through our changes. We are important to each other; we enjoy sharing our lives. I look forward to her letters the way I anticipate spending time with other friends. It is comforting to know that someone on another continent, in another country, cares. Ultimately, we all need, and we all want, someone to hear about our heavy burdens and wonder how we are pulling the wagons of life.

—*Karen Hindhede*

Friendship makes prosperity more shining
and lessens adversity by dividing
and sharing it.

—MARCUS TULLIUS CICERO

Scented Notepaper

We send personal letters so infrequently these days, why not make it that much more special for our friend on the receiving end? You can add a personal touch to your letters by scenting your stationery. It's incredibly easy. These instructions should make enough for you and to give as gifts to friends.

8 ounces unscented talcum powder

15 drops of your favorite essential oil

6 small, closely woven cotton or silk bags, open on one side (available at craft stores)

ribbon

notepaper and envelopes

a box large enough to hold notepaper

1 large plastic bag

In a nonmetallic bowl, combine the powder and essential oils. Cover tightly and let sit for a day. Spoon the mixture into the bags and tie with ribbon. Place the cloth bags in-between the layers of notepaper and envelopes in the box, and put the box into the plastic bag. Cover tightly and allow to sit for a few days, so that the scent will permeate the paper. Makes 6 sachets.

The Best Medicine

I am at work. I hate my job. I hate my boss. I hate my husband. I am fat. I need one thing, my best friend. She's 5,000 miles away and probably right in the middle of dinner with her family. I dial the phone. She answers. A quiet sigh of relief escapes me. She immediately asks, "What's wrong?" She always knows.

I tell her of all my hates. She tells me she too hates her husband, her job, her boss, and her flab. I knew she would understand.

We discover we've both been thinking about going back to school. She's considering becoming a masseuse. I laugh and say I've been thinking about esthetician school. We ponder a name for our spa where we will always be surrounded by happy people, nice music, and wonderful smells. There will be no pressure of meetings, presentations, or deadlines. We go on for five more minutes about what treatments our spa would offer, both knowing it will never happen.

We then discuss our two-faced bosses, who expect us to work 10–12 hour days, regardless of whether we have something else to do. We are certain they enjoy being at work because they have nothing else, and this allows them to ignore their loneliness. We know they really just want us there to keep them company.

We wonder how our husbands can be so clueless. We question why it has to be an ongoing drama to get them to help clean up. We can't figure out why it even has to be a discussion. They don't have to ask *us* to put away the dishes in the dishwasher. They don't have to plead with *us* to throw away expired milk. We just do it.

Yes, we then decide, we are both gluttons. Neither of us has any discipline. We want to be skinny and sexy. But we really like food. She confesses she ate two éclairs yesterday for breakfast. I tell her I ate two slices of cheesecake before bed last night. We conclude it's okay we are fifteen pounds away from a size 8. We agree that we will never be twenty-one again.

I hear the screams in the background indicating that her two boys are fighting. She ignores them, but I don't. I realize I am cured. She is the medicine that cannot be duplicated. This was a record healing, only eighteen minutes of gab time. I tell her I have to go back to work.

I smile to myself. I can live with my job. I feel sorry for my boss. I love my husband. I'm healthy and enjoy food.

—*Ginger Couden*

A faithful friend is the medicine of life.

—Ecclesiasticus 6:16

Friendship is Spelled with a P

After writing her "Cheery, Cheery Checklist" on the black-board, Ms. Lorimer turned to face the class to make sure we had taken note that the assignment was due no later than Friday.

Usually we didn't get assigned actual work on the first day of school, but Ms. Lorimer was definitely not your usual teacher. She was prone to repeating words for effect and wearing dramatic garb, and she had a perfectly picked "fro" that served to blur the chalk on the board every time she turned to face her class of first graders. Her mantra was learning is fun, fun, fun! I turned to catch Scott's eye, but he was otherwise occupied making goofy faces with the other students whose last names were closer to Parker.

So far, the first day of school was a letdown. Scott and I must have ridden our bikes 500 miles that summer. We alternated weekends staying over at each other's house, and even stayed up late and watched *Saturday Night Live* one weekend, pretending to laugh with the babysitter, and later laughing for real at how stupid the show seemed.

Today summer seemed a million years ago.

Scott knew people from his T-ball team and from his church group. He seemed to know everybody at the big school, and he had very little time for me. Maybe I would be acknowledged on the bus ride home; I hoped I would. When I climbed on board, Scott was in the packed "popular and bad kids" section at the back of the bus, and I had to sit at the front where there was still space. The back of my neck burned, and the burning rose to the tips of my ears.

Before the bus left the circular drive of the elementary school, there was a commotion at the back of the bus. One student screamed in horror, which was soon drowned out by laughter, and more laughter.

I turned to see what the excitement was about, and saw that all eyes seemed to be on Scott, whose head was lowered. He was not smiling for the first time that day.

One of the older kids, maybe from fourth grade, was chanting "Pee-pee Parker," and other kids were joining in. Despite the bus driver's shouts for everyone to settle down, I got up and made my way to where Scott was sitting. His pants were darkened, and liquid was pooling on the green vinyl of the seat. Without a second thought, I sat down in the pee next to my friend.

It's been decades since that moment, but it remains vivid in my memory—the pleasure of loyalty.

—*James G. Campbell*

And a youth said, Speak to us of Friendship.

And he answered, saying:

Your friend is your needs answered.

He is your field which you sow with love and reap with thanksgiving.

And he is your board and your fireside.

For you come to him with your hunger, and you seek him for peace.

—KAHLIL GIBRAN

The Right Moment

I woke up with a headache, a backache, and a serious case of PMS. The Midol wasn't helping, and I was alone in my apartment with piles of laundry and a graduate thesis to do. Luckily for him, my live-in boyfriend had left for work an hour earlier. But since then I hadn't been able to get back to sleep, with my temples and ovaries throbbing. I propped a pillow under my knees and stared at the wall, moodily crying and downing painkillers for three hours that morning, and waiting for the pain to abate so that I could do some housework, or even just sit at my computer and type a few more pages about psychoanalytic linguistic theory and Asian-American literature. The threat of my impending deadline only made the PMS more stubborn, as if my hormones were saying, "I'm not going to be rushed, and I'm not going to be ignored."

When the phone rang I answered it greedily, expecting a telemarketer on whom I could take out some of my frustration. Instead it was Lezlie, my dearest friend from graduate school. She sensed my foul temper immediately and told me to forget about my paper and my dishes and my boyfriend. "Your body is talking to you, Brookie." An hour later she was leading me into her tiny basement apartment, her arm linked in mine. She had made a makeshift bed on the floor with layers of incredibly soft homemade quilts surrounded by pillows.

After tucking me in, she brought us a tray of chamomile and

ginseng teas, which are supposed to relieve cramps, a huge bowl of popcorn, and a plate of chocolate. She covered my aching tummy with a warm rice heating pad. Therapeutic lavender candles burned nearby. As I settled in, she played the video *When Harry Met Sally*, so that I would have an excuse to cry. Unexpectedly, my body, tensed to ward off the next wave of cramps, finally began to relax, and I gradually drifted off to sleep. I knew then that all the lavender, ginseng, and chocolate in the world would have made no difference if I'd been home alone, waiting for unsuspecting telemarketers; and I have no doubt that the real remedy was the unselfish kindness of my best friend.

—*Brooke Barnett*

Ah, how good it feels . . . the hand of
an old friend.

—Mary Englebright

Customized Candles

To thank a friend for lighting the way when life seemed so dark, consider candles. You can make beautiful candles at a fraction of the cost of buying the decorated versions (and, of course, you can make these for yourself as well). Here are some elegant, yet unbelievably easy ways to decorate candles:

Purchase some plain votive candles, some straight glasses, some sheets of Japanese rice paper (you know, the ones that have flowers and leaves embedded), and raffia. Place the candles in the glasses, cut the paper to fit, wrap the paper around the glass, and tie the paper on with raffia. To finish off, you can add a leaf or dried flower to the raffia.

Decorate pillar candles with attractive nail heads (available at hardware stores). Choose nails not longer than ⅛ inch, and press gently into candles to avoid cracking.

Roll white candles in a plate of silver or gold glitter. No glue needed! Or apply glitter to the tops of floating candles. Cover the wicks with tape, spray the tops of the candles with spray adhesive, sprinkle with glitter, then remove the tape.

Decorate the little metal cases around votives by placing white glue around the outside and rolling in glitter.

Start with plain candles and apply stickers or temporary tattoos in a pleasing pattern. Or try bindis—traditional Indian face decorations that stick on almost anything.

Try gold and silver leaf. It attaches itself easily to the surface of a candle and gives an elegant look.

Buy a few clear glass candle pots. Add water, to which you've added a few drops of food coloring to create the color you want, then float a candle in each pot.

Inexpensive bangle bracelets can be placed around the bottom of fat candles. Or tie on ribbon, or glue on sequins. Or string beads or buttons on a piece of thin wire and wrap around a candle's base. Just make sure whatever you choose does not come into contact with the flame.

Welcome Home

"Welcome Home, Carey and Dena!" the note on our front door read. "What's this?" I asked, while my hubby, Carey, just grinned. As we stepped into our tiny apartment, my mouth hung open. The place was sparkling—not an ounce of clutter or dust anywhere.

It was one-thirty a.m. First-year seminary students, Carey and I had spent every day for six months working at our day jobs—Carey at a campus bookstore, and me in the seminary public relations office—then wolfing down fast food in the car while driving to rehearsals for a Christian theater production.

Ironically, this week was called "hell week" by the cast, since we were only a few days from the show's opening. The 150-member cast and crew spent evenings from seven to eleven p.m. (or later) going over our movements, getting costumes fitted, and practicing our scenes.

Each day, we had guzzled caffeine at our day jobs and told ourselves it would only last a few more nights. Exhausted and yet exhilarated, Carey and I assured each other we'd clean our house and car later . . . after we were back in the land of the living.

Dropping my bag, I walked through the crackerbox kitchen, noticing that the dishes were done—by hand, since we didn't have a dishwasher—and the linoleum had been swept and mopped. Even the living room floor had been vacuumed.

"Who did this?" I asked Carey. He shrugged and laughed.

I made my way into the bedroom, where the bed had been made. A note, taped to the pillow, read: "Enjoy, you lovebirds!"

"It was Andrea and Lee, wasn't it?" I asked. "She must have borrowed the key from you."

Carey nodded. "She asked me for it yesterday, but she wouldn't tell me what she was up to—only that they and the Hartigs were planning a surprise."

Lee and Andrea Chitwood and Jason and Sharon Hartig, our best friends, were two young married couples from our church. "This is incredible!" I exclaimed. "Our friends are so thoughtful."

Carey yawned. "Yes, it was," he agreed, limping toward the bed. He was in his pajamas, with his head on the pillow, before I could blink.

"We'll thank them in the morning," I said, knowing they probably wouldn't appreciate a two A.M. wakeup call—even from two extremely grateful friends.

George Eliot once said, "What do we live for if it is not to make life less difficult for each other?" During that extremely busy season of life, my best friends taught me that simple acts of kindness (often unasked for, and many times undeserved) are the sweetest pleasures of all.

—*Dena J. Dyer*

The balm of life, a kind and
faithful friend.

—MERCY OTIS WARREN

A Helping Hand

As most of my friends know, I am not ever going to win an award for my organizational skills. That's why it was great when my friend Mary presented me with a personalized address book. Not only did she pen in all the addresses, phone numbers, and e-mail addresses of the friends we share, she arrived at my house one evening with a bottle of wine in hand. She asked me for my old tattered address book, made sense of all the papers sticking out of its binder, and patiently sat and compiled the old with the new. Her gift is one that keeps on giving, allowing me to stay connected to those I care about.

—*Mary Beth Sammons*

Hold a true friend with both hands.

—NIGERIAN PROVERB

The Vow

Our lives are complicated by the responsibilities of marriage, children, and careers. It's not easy balancing everything on our plates. A phone call from a friend on a lazy Sunday afternoon helps us to temporarily escape preparations for another busy week. We've cooked enough chicken, beef, and gravy to carry us through a few "heat and eat" meals. Clean clothes wait on top of the dryer, to be delivered to our loved ones by the Laundry Fairy. We just want to talk about our crow's feet, and make a solemn vow to have our eyes "done" when we're fifty-five. We'll pretend that we are going off on a spa weekend, and will come back thoroughly tightened and tucked. We'll look rested and rejuvenated, and will go to our graves with this secret. Our husbands tell us that we look "wonderful just the way we are," but we know better. We're closer than sisters in many ways, without the emotional baggage of family history. We want nothing from each other but the opportunity to be friends of the heart. It's simple, and a pleasure to boot.

—*Robin E. Woods*

When the chips are down, there's nothing
like a good girlfriend . . . someone who
accepts you—warts, wrinkles, weight,
and all—unconditionally.

—Barbara Jenkins

Hungary Water

Cheer up a friend with good smells. This lovely floral water
was first created in 1370 for Queen Elizabeth of Hungary. It's a
great blend of spicy fragrances. Just put in a lovely glass bottle
with a ribbon, and you've got a unique gift for that special
friend.

20 drops lemon essential oil

20 drops melissa essential oil

20 drops peppermint essential oil

20 drops rosemary essential oil

⅓ cup ethyl alcohol

Blend the essential oils together in a glass bowl. Add the
alcohol and pour into glass bottles. Makes approximately
½ cup.

The Road Trip

Donelyn, DeDe, and I take a road trip twice a year to get away from it all and celebrate our friendship. We never go very far from home, as it's not the location that is important. We usually rent a hotel room near by, order room service, and completely relax. We talk, listen, laugh, and catch up on each other's lives while placing our family and work responsibilities temporarily aside.

The three of us have been close friends for a long time. We understand each other whether we are shining in our best light or standing in the dark looking quite dim. Our friendship is that simple . . . and that complex.

So when Donelyn called out of the blue and mapped out the plans for an impromptu outing, I immediately said, "Count me in! I'll be there."

Two days later, the three of us cleared our work and family schedules and were cruising down the highway in Donelyn's van. Absorbed in conversation, we hardly noticed the perfect spring weather outside. Not a cloud was in the sky, except for a fleeting shadow that flickered inside the van as we rounded the last corner to our destination. Pulling into the parking lot, we gathered up our belongings, locked the van doors, and walked through the building entrance.

Exchanging brief smiles, we clasped hands and waited patiently at the check-in counter. "May I help you?" the receptionist queried.

"Yes," DeDe answered. "We're here for my first chemother-apy treatment."

—*Tamela Meredith Partridge*

The most valuable things in life are not measured in monetary terms. The really important things are not houses and lands, stocks and bonds, automobiles and real estate, but friendships, trust, confidence, empathy, mercy, love and faith.

—Russell V. DeLong

Personalized Presents

Support a friend going through chemo by throwing a hat shower. Everyone brings a hat and an inspirational letter. (This and the next idea come from *Gifts with Heart* by Mary Beth Sammons, which is chock-full of meaningful gift ideas.)

Cheer up a friend with the winter blues by sending a big box in February that is filled with 28 little wrapped presents—one to open for each day of the month. The gifts can be small—a pack of gum, a silly refrigerator magnet.

Create a book from friends for someone's special decade birthday. Ask everyone who knows your friend to write something about why she or he is special. Collect in a large blank book.

Have flowers delivered for no reason.

Send a card to an old friend you've been out of touch with, telling her that you've been thinking of her.

Got a housebound friend? Bring the world to him or her. Create a Parisian weekend, a Greek holiday, a Chinese junket, with the appropriate food, décor, music, and videos. If you want assistance, check out *Weekends Away (Without Leaving Home)* by the Editors of Conari Press.

LOVE AND LEARNING

Friendship is love with understanding.

—ANONYMOUS

Friends are witnesses, confidantes, fellow travelers on the journey of life. They know our deepest secrets, understand us sometimes better than even we do. We don't just go through life with
them; we grow in and through their presence. That's why, in so
many ways, it is the love of our friends that makes much of life
worth living.

———————————————————

A Good Book Shared

She's my pseudo big sister, my wise muse, and guardian angel. But most importantly, my friend Lin is my self-help reading companion. There is not one book on living life to the fullest, deciphering men, finding abundance, or learning to run with the wolves that Lin and I have not dissected in our fifteen-year friendship. We met while attending a medical meeting at the Del Coronado Hotel in San Diego in 1987, and have remained the closest of friends despite two career changes (mine), four failed relationships (mine), and a cross-country move (me again).

During our hour-long monthly phone calls, Lin and I cover the routine questions with respectful interest as we rush to get to what we call "the good stuff." Invariably, the good stuff is peppered with the lessons learned from a self-help book currently on one of our nightstands. At the moment, Lin is reading *The Power of Now* and working on her perpetual struggle to live in the present. I am reading *Consider the Butterfly* and learning to look for meaningful coincidences. Lin and I often joke that we have overdosed on self-help books and come full circle with the principles and theories they espouse. But even if we recognize that we have cycled through our minimalist phase more than once, and that we have evolved beyond "the rules" all on our own, thank you, it is still nice to chatter away with someone who appreciates your love of reading.

—*Gwen Mayes*

Some friendships are made by nature,
some by contract, some by interest
and some by souls.

—JEREMY TAYLOR

The Most Precious Thing

There is a couple that comes to the café every so often. He leads her carefully to their normal table. Once the woman accidentally bumped into me as I refilled my coffee cup. "So sorry," said the gentleman quietly. I looked down at his hand. No ring. Curious, I asked, "Your wife?" "No," he responded, his pale eyes twinkling, "a good friend."

They sit close together, their chairs touching. Both are bent over with age, yet well groomed. He adjusts her wrap around her shoulders, feeds her a bite of food. She seems unaware of her surroundings. He makes sure to offer her sips of water between each bite. Each move is so gentle, so heart-inspired. She isn't a burden to him, but his friend. He cares for her as if she is the most precious thing he has ever come across.

He loves her, no matter that she can't communicate it back. But maybe she can. Maybe there is a small light in her eyes that he alone can see. He could tell what she needed even though she seemed unaware of his efforts.

Friendship: knowing what the other needs without prompting, support when others have given up on you, treating you as a treasure, not a burden.

—*Ellen Nordberg*

Friendship is a sheltering tree.

—COLERIDGE

Be a Friend

Springtime in New York City—my first apartment, a new job, and a new girlfriend—life was simply wonderful. I felt so good I decided to share my happiness with someone less fortunate. So I called The Lighthouse for the Blind. The volunteer coordinator explained they needed help with an outreach program for elderly, recently blind shut-ins. I thought, "I can do that." She assigned me to someone named Charley.

The night before my first meeting with Charley, my girlfriend and I had a big fight. She left; I sulked. The next morning found me dragging myself to meet "the shut-in," my generous mood evaporated. I'd spent the night reliving the fight, unable to sleep. Cranky and soaked with self-pity, I remember thinking, "I'd rather have a root canal than visit some old blind man."

Charley lived in a rough neighborhood. Dodging delirious

winos, occasionally crossing the street to avoid desperate-looking drug addicts, I trudged toward our first meeting. I tried to imagine what he'd look like. The coordinator said he was very old. At that time I considered anyone sixty-five to be ready for The Dirt Nap. Charley, I'd been told, was older than that. "Great," I muttered on my wino-strewn walk, "he's probably senile." I promised myself that after this one visit, I'd call the Lighthouse and weasel out of my commitment.

I climbed the crumbling steps to Charley's sixth-floor apartment and banged on his metal door. There were shuffling sounds. The door opened a few inches. A face appeared in the narrow chained gap. I gasped. "This guy's older than God!" I thought. Cataract-clouded eyes, wispy white hair, Charley seemed ancient.

Ushering me into his apartment, Charley invited me to sit on his sofa. He reminded me of my grandfather, who had died years before. My grandfather had been like a buddy, telling me stories, listening to my problems, never lecturing me. Being with Charley reminded me how much I missed him.

Small talk soon became biography. Charley told me how he'd lost his vision and his wife of more than fifty years in the last few months. And how he'd outlived all his friends. But he said it without a trace of self-pity.

As I tried to imagine how he must feel, Charley explained how fortunate he'd been to have such a wonderful marriage, a lifelong friendship. And then, as if sensing my uneasiness, he smiled.

Time slipped by. My agreed-upon one-hour visit stretched to three. By the time I left him that afternoon, my self-pity had vanished. Charley soon became more than a volunteer "project." In fact, visits with my new friend became the high point of my week. Charley's stories always put things in perspective.

Until I met Charley I approached people only thinking about what they could do for me. "If you want a friend, be a friend," Charley said—a lesson that's stayed with me ever since that spring day in New York City so many years ago.

—*Bill Asenjo*

No birth certificate is issued when
friendship is born. There is nothing tangible.
There is just a feeling that your life is
and that your capacity to love and care
has miraculously been enlarged with out
any effort on your part. It's like having a
tiny apartment and somebody moves in
with you. But instead of becoming
cramped and crowded, the space
expands, and you discover rooms you
never knew you had until your
friend moved in with you.

—STEVE TESICH

Frangipani Sachet Powder

Thank a friend for being in your life with this fabulous scent. It is the formula of a famous Italian alchemist, Muzio Frangipani, who invented this recipe centuries ago. How many this makes depends on the size of your sachet bags. A description of how to make sachet bags follows the recipe.

3 cups orrisroot powder

1 cup sandalwood powder

1 cup vetiver powder

5 drops sandalwood essential oil

5 drops rose essential oil

5 drops neroli essential oil

Combine all ingredients. Stir and let sit out for a few days. Use to fill sachets. Makes 5 cups.

Simple Sachets

Sachets are little scented cloth bags used to impart fragrance to your drawers or closets. Many women place them between items of lingerie or nightgowns. Traditionally they are made of light cotton so that the aroma can come through. You might try a tightly woven cotton lace or some other beautiful pattern.

> fabric scraps at least 4 inches by 8 inches each
>
> ribbons

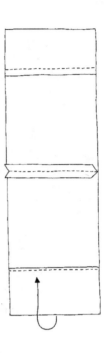

Cut fabric into two 4-inch by 8-inch rectangles. On each piece, fold down one of the 4-inch sides 2 inches, patterned side out, and stitch—this fold is the top of the sachet. Pin the pieces of fabric together, patterned side in, and stitch together the bottom and sides. (See diagram.)

Turn patterned side out, fill the sachet half full, and use the ribbon to create a drawstring close at the top.

Zillions of Zinnias

Fifteen years ago, my best friend Ann and I prepared a meal for an older couple in our community. As we delivered the meal, we paused to admire the husband's zinnias. Despite his age and weakening health, Mr. Flynn successfully cultivated a bed of zinnias each year. And what a beautiful zinnia garden it was! A rainbow of color, the bed extended the length of his driveway.

"Let's get you some flowers to take home," he said, noting our appreciation. A fondness of flowers was one of many interests Ann and I shared. No wonder we became friends when she moved to town.

As we talked, I learned that Mr. Flynn had grown his zinnias from seed. "You can save the old flowers for next year's seed," he said, as he clipped a bouquet and handed it to me.

He led Ann and me into his garage. "Look at this," he said, picking up a big box of dried zinnia flowers. "You have to keep the old flowers cut back if you want to get lots of blooms," he explained. He got two bags, filled them with zinnia seeds, and instructed us to plant them the next spring.

By spring, Ann had moved away—ten hours away. Within several years, Mr. Flynn was gone too. Some years later, my husband and I visited Ann and her family in Mississippi. As Ann and I walked through her yard, I saw a small patch of zinnias. "Remember Mr. Flynn's zinnias?" I asked.

Ann laughed. "These are from Mr. Flynn's zinnias," she said. "Do you still have some?" I was ashamed to admit that mine had fizzled out. I had been less diligent than she in keeping seeds each year. "We'll just have to send you home with some seeds," Ann said.

A single seed goes a long way, I thought. It can carry flowers and joy from North Carolina to Mississippi and back to North Carolina again. Not only had our friendship endured Ann's move, but so had Mr. Flynn's zinnias and our memory of this gentle man. These were surely friendship flowers.

—Julia Taylor Ebel

The essence of true friendship is to make
allowances for another's little lapses.

—DAVID STOREY

Seed Exchange

There's great pleasure in sharing seeds and plants with friends who are gardeners, not the least of which is knowing that a bit of your green thumb is brightening up their world as well. To send seeds, shake the flower heads over an empty jar, then pour the contents of the jar into small envelopes. Seal the envelopes shut, write on the outside the name of the flower and how to grow it, then mail in a padded envelope. A sweet surprise!

Spreading Sunshine

Shirley introduces me to waitresses all over town. "Beverly," she'll say, reading the name tag of the waitress serving us. "I'm Shirley and this is my friend Jan. How *are* you?" She speaks as if we're all at a dinner party. It's not that Shirley is the Patron Saint of Restaurant Workers, or even a waitress herself. It's just that she knows how to celebrate a person. We're all human beings, aren't we, sharing this interesting moment together, even if she and I are wedged in a booth, and Beverly is carrying a coffeepot?

Sometimes the chosen waitress will look puzzled, perhaps waiting for a complaint or Candid Camera. More often, her eyes soften and her shoulders drop their burdens. Occasionally, during a meal, the restaurant manager will bend intimately over our table and ask us how everything is, as if we're very important eaters or food critics.

The first time Shirley said her restaurant hello, I felt uncomfortable. This wasn't proper server–diner etiquette. Why would a waitress want to know my name? I'm not famous. Let the woman get on with her business, for heaven's sake, and let us get on with our own private talking.

But there's something about Shirley's heart that shakes a person and her old, stale notions. "This is abundance, isn't it?" Shirley will say, exhaling deeply, surveying our feast of cheeses and chocolates and teas. Her overflowing gratitude, her practice of honoring just who is sharing any given moment with her, is so contagious that I'm sure all the other diners are answering "Yes," without even knowing the question. When the feast is through, she often finds her way to the kitchen, stopping just this side of the open door, so she can personally thank the chef without violating any health codes.

Make no mistake, Shirley isn't Pollyanna. She has faced the raw, harsh places of life. To bed at two years old with no food. Singing to keep the bears away while walking alone and terrified in the backwoods of Nova Scotia. Running away from home at thirteen. Somehow, instead of hardening and twisting inward, she has remained open. "How's your heart?" she'll ask, and all the stories, all the mundane details I've saved up to entertain her with, melt away as I go straight to the core. She can take it, whether I'm feeling depressed, cranky, ecstatic, or whimsical. My words aren't lost in a flurry of her own thoughts. Neither are they torn apart and analyzed. Shirley listens as if my words are all children running to her, clamoring for attention. She hugs the energy behind them and sends them back to me. I am left feeling nurtured and freed by wonder at this goofy, mysterious world.

"How human," she says simply. "Thank you for telling me what's true for you. Wait, here are some index cards you can carry around with you, and every time you want to thank someone you can just leave them a little note."

Consider this an index card for you, Shirley.

—*Jan Henrikson*

The happiest moments of my life have
been the flow of affection among friends.

—THOMAS JEFFERSON

The Gift

It was our tenth wedding anniversary and, months before, I had planned a weekend getaway to a luxurious spa. My friend Rebecca had volunteered to stay with the kids, and all the arrangements had been made. By the time the weekend rolled around, though, our financial situation had changed. My husband's job was in jeopardy, and it made no sense to spend a lot of money on pampering. I poured out my disappointment to Rebecca, who encouraged me to go somewhere anyway. I scaled back, choosing the cheapest room in an inexpensive hotel an hour away. Off my husband and I went.

When we arrived, we discovered that Rebecca had called and gotten us a suite, courtesy of her, and the concierge wanted to know when we would like to book our side-by-side massages, also a gift from her. Not only did she watch our kids, but she paid for the entire weekend, including the bottle of chilled champagne that was waiting as we opened the door to our beautiful suite. Due to Rebecca's love and generosity, the weekend was a dream come true.

—*Stephanie Matthews*

The verb "to love" in Persian is "to have
a friend." "I love you" translated literally
is "I have you as a friend."

—SHUSHA GUPPY

Miniature Topiary

This tiny artificial tree makes a wonderful thank-you or anniversary gift for a friend with a big heart but no green thumb. And it can be made in a matter of minutes.

> miniature ceramic or wooden pot
> small rock to fit in pot
> floral foam
> hot-glue gun and glue sticks
> 4 small twigs, cut to equal lengths
> small artificial pine garland
> dried berries

Place the rock in the bottom of the pot to create stability. Cut a piece of floral foam to fit in the pot. Glue the foam into the pot.

Insert three or four twigs in the center of the foam, to create the "trunk" of the topiary. Glue the trunk to the foam at the base.

Cut a small piece of pine garland off and glue it around the base of the trunk, to hide the foam. Form a ball by winding the pine garland until it is the right size for the topiary. Glue the ball to the top of the twigs. Glue berries to make a pleasing design. Makes 1.

I'll Pick You Up

After seven years of marriage, I was about to become a father. One day the seriousness of it all just overwhelmed me, and I called my friend Duane. "What are you doing after work?" I asked. "Nothing," he said. "What's up?"

Duane and I had been friends since fourth grade. We had gone to high school and college together, stood in each other's weddings, and seen each other at our best and worst. I said without hesitation, "Fatherhood, man. I'm scared."

"Okay," he said. "I'll pick you up."

He drove me to a park near where we had grown up in Buffalo and listened as I unloaded all my fears and worries. Suppose I wasn't ready for fatherhood? How would it change my life, my marriage? What if I was lousy at it? What if I lost my job? What if the baby had a congenital illness or disability? What if . . .

"Gary," he said when I had finished summoning every concern in my imagination, "you're one of the smartest people I know. You think everything through. You'll do what everybody does their first time as a parent. You'll try something. If it doesn't work, you'll try something else, and keep trying till it feels right. You're going to be a good father because you're a good person, a good teacher, and a good friend. And you're not doing it alone. You've got a wife and family and friends. It won't always be easy, but in the long run it will be okay."

That day, as any good friend would, Duane listened. Then

he offered just the right amount of support and reassurance. Soon thereafter, my wife gave birth to a beautiful baby girl, and now, twenty-five years later, my daughter, visiting home, just peeked in and saw me working on this piece. Now she is upstairs soaking in the tub, completely unaware of the role her godfather played in preparing me for her arrival.

One year after our trip to the park, Duane called me at work. "What's going on?" I asked. "The baby's coming soon," Duane said. "I'm scared."

"I'll pick you up."

> Friendship is unnecessary, like
> philosophy, like art. . . . It has no survival
> value; rather it is one of those things that
> give value to survival.
>
> —C. S. LEWIS

True Companion

You'd think I'd have gained some tolerance for my friend's sleeping habits after fifteen years, but no. Always furious when woken, cold and disoriented, by amorous nudges, I've been verbally abusive and at times even pushed her out of bed. She slept alone on the sofa after these mishaps. *Hasta luego*! I guess she felt I should be used to her advances. Talk about a slow learner!

When I wake at night, I check my blood sugar. I've been an insulin-dependent diabetic for nearly forty years, with many low-blood-sugar parties with the paramedics en route to the ER. When I've been dangerously low, I've wondered if aggravation had anything to do with it. My partner just let me take care of myself, not wanting to increase my wrath.

Diabetic problems escalate at night. My blood sugars often go life-threateningly low, as evidenced by rebounding highs. For fifteen years, she monitored my diabetes, noticing minute changes in the way I moved, my breathing, even how I smelled. If she sensed I was going low, she pestered me into consciousness. For fifteen years I cursed her and threw her out of bed. And the next night she'd do it again.

She died a few months ago of kidney failure. I was heartbroken and surprised to find I missed our nocturnal adventures. Kiku, my cat, taught me true friends don't always take the easy route.

—*D. De Mink*

It's funny how dogs and cats know
the inside of folks better than
other folks do, isn't it?

—ELEANOR H. PORTER

Unconditional Love

My friend Robert and I go out for lunch once a month. Robert is very big. His bear hugs literally sweep you off your feet and take your breath away. One day, when we were heading out for our monthly outing, Robert announced that his birthday was soon.

"How old are ya gonna be?" I asked.

He bashfully said, "Thirty-nine. I'm an old man."

"Yes, you are!" I agreed.

Robert's body may be almost forty. His mind, however, stopped growing around age four; his mental skills are about kindergarten level. Going out for lunch with me is one of the highlights of his month.

Elvis Presley's "Oh Let Me Be Your Teddy Bear" is "our" song. And like a bear cub, Robert can be playful one minute and very angry the next. Our conversation routinely revolves around what I am going to cook for dinner that night, whether I went shopping yesterday, and whether I will take a nap after I take him

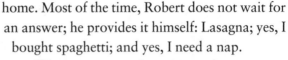

home. Most of the time, Robert does not wait for an answer; he provides it himself: Lasagna; yes, I bought spaghetti; and yes, I need a nap.

Wherever we go, he seems to know everybody. And if he doesn't, he will introduce himself: "Hi, I'm Robert. What's your name? Are you going shopping? What are eating for dinner tonight? Probably lasagna?"

Most people smile and answer politely. After lunch we usually go to the store. He likes to buy cards for his friends. He works at Goodwill during the week, making football helmets, so he always has some money. He is fortunate that his parents are alive and very actively involved in his life. However, they are getting older and exhausted from caring for him.

There really is no name for Robert's disability. His mom once told me that was the hardest thing to accept. He has physical problems such as club feet, lupus, and a heart condition. His eyes are a bit protruding; one look at him, and most people immediately identify him as "retarded."

So why do I cherish my friendship with Robert? Robert loves me unconditionally. He loves me whether I go out for lunch with him or cancel at the last moment. He loves me whether I just spent hours at a beauty parlor or open the door with uncombed hair, bad breath, and makeup from last night smeared all over my face. And he never noticed the twenty pounds I kept on after my last child's birth.

When I come home from church on Sunday afternoons, there is always an envelope with crudely cut coupons and a plate of cookies on my porch. On special occasions there will also be a card and a little gadget from the dollar store. His dad drives him around every Sunday because Robert has several friends that he makes such deliveries to. Could there be a more rewarding friendship?

—Heide A. W. Kaminski

True friendship is seen through the heart,
not through the eyes.

—Anonymous

God's Grace

I was really low. Divorce had separated me from my children, and I felt an acute sense of loss. Somehow, despair turned to resolve. I'd always intended to work on my garden but never found the time. It was now or never.

A riot of grass and weeds mocked me. The ground was heavy clay, and the spade grew heavier with every load I dug. With a sigh, I stopped for a rest, gazing enviously over the fence to where flowers of all descriptions competed for the best display. It seemed so perfect.

Suddenly, the old lady whose garden it was appeared, looking at me. We'd never spoken to each other much before. Her kind face framed the softest of brown eyes, and her smile was warm. Returning her gaze, I felt an empathy that seemed very real.

She held a thermos flask and offered me coffee. Her voice was so soothing. "You like my garden? God's grace, I call it. I'm Milly by the way. Don't let the coffee go cold. I'm glad to see you out here, at last, but you seem a bit lost, somehow. Can I help?"

Hesitantly, I replied, "Your ground is so fertile, compared to mine. This clay's so wet and heavy, nothing nice could grow in it, so what magic did you use?"

She laughed and invited me over. She led me to the corner, pointing at an enormous, wooden box, open-topped, and filled with soft, brown earth. "Put your hands into it," she instructed.

"Hold two handfuls to your face, and take a deep sniff!"

I did as I was told. The compost felt so good, in my fingers, alive with insects of all kinds, and there was a smell of life about it, invigorating and so natural. Nothing I'd experienced before came close to that feeling of communion with nature. She smiled at my expression, knowing I was hooked.

"This is what my garden needs?" I asked, knowing the answer already. "How do I go about getting it?"

Thus began a friendship, and an education, that was to last a lifetime. Her lifelong love of nature transmitted itself to me like a benign contagion. She had no family still living and spent her time gardening. Her knowledge was vast, and her patient faith a real inspiration to me. Life, she said, was a precious gift, not to be wasted on regrets or self-recrimination.

Milly brought purpose back into my life. Nature has so much beauty to bestow, if only you take time to accept it. My favorite daily moment is still plunging my hands deep into the compost. I believe God was watching on the day we met across the garden fence. That's why she'll never be just Milly to me. I'll always think of her as "God's grace."

—*Tony Leather*

No love, no friendship
can cross the path of our destiny
without leaving some mark on it forever.

—François Mauriac

Painted Pots

Brighten up a plant lover's home with one-of-a-kind flower pots with decorated rims. Because the clay in the terra-cotta absorbs some of the color, you will end up with a matte effect. If you do a number of pots of various sizes and use complementary colors, they will look great when clustered together. Because of the terra-cotta, green and yellow look particularly striking.

terra-cotta flowerpots, any size

pencil

tape measure

small paintbrush

assorted ceramic enamels

Let your imagination go wild. You can paint the pot bodies one color and the rims another. Or make polka dots in a contrasting color to the rim. Or try vertical stripes by marking lines in pencil after measuring with a tape measure. Or try vertical zigzags interspersed with dots. Combine some solid color pots with ones with designs. Let dry.

The Great Catalyst

I call Michelle "The Great Catalyst" because she's wrought so much change in my life and given me so many gifts in the four years that I've known her. The first gift she gave me was one of persistence. Everyday, Michelle would bounce around the corner at work and say a big "hi" despite my leave-me-the-heck-alone expression. I'd roll my eyes toward her cubicle, hoping she'd get the hint to leave. Instead, she'd smile even more broadly and perkily ask how my weekend or evening had been. I'd grunt an answer to shut her up, and eventually she'd slink toward her desk, only to cheerily return the next day.

At the time, her persistence felt like another of the many burdens I was already bearing—my grandmother's slow death from stroke complications, out-of-the blue financial problems, and health issues that sapped both my physical and emotional energy. In the end, however, her willingness to reach out to me proved to be one of the best gifts I've ever received. I felt utterly alone during that time and needed to know that someone, even a stranger at my new job, cared.

—*Pamela D. Blackmon*

The bird a nest, the spider a web,
man friendship.

—WILLIAM BLAKE

A Gift of Love

The phone rang. It was my dearest friend, Ruth. She said, "You have to come over. I got something for you today." Ruth was one for surprises and acts of kindness, so I had no idea what it could be this time.

Later that day, I walked in Ruth's back door, and hanging there in the kitchen was the most gorgeous wedding dress I had ever seen. Ruth stood there smiling. "I was shopping in town," she explained, "and in the window of a consignment shop hung this dress."

Tears sprang to my eyes. My wedding was in two months, and I had yet to find a dress. I just couldn't afford to go out and buy one, so I had been hoping and praying that something would come up.

"Go to the bathroom and try it on," said Ruth.

I looked at it and thought, "There is no way that it will fit me. But it is so beautiful, maybe it just looks small." I got the dress down over my head and worked it down over my hips but it wouldn't zip up. I came out of the bathroom and asked Ruth to help me.

It wouldn't zip. I could have just cried at that point. I had so wanted that dress to fit. Ruth said, "Well, we will just keep looking," then offered to give me money toward a gown. This really got me to crying, because my mother hadn't even offered to help with anything for the wedding, and here was a friend offering to help.

Now I was standing there in the too-small gown, crying. Ruth said, "Stop or you will get the dress wet, and then you'll have to buy it and wear it, back hanging out and all!"

I knew she was just being gruff with me to avoid crying herself. But we couldn't get the dress off. I was stuck! Ruth's daughter walked in, and there we were, me bent over and Ruth trying to pull this gown off me. We all began to laugh. Before I knew it, the three of us were on the floor, laughing as if we had heard the best joke ever.

After much prying, we did get the dress off without ripping it, and I did end up finding a wedding dress, but that memory of Ruth's dress and her kindness will stick with me forever.

—*Joeanne Steras*

The greatest healing therapy is
friendship and love.

—HUBERT HUMPHREY

Friendship Treasure Box

Surprise a dear friend with a treasure box that com-
memorates your friendship. Find or buy a beautiful
box. Fill it with photos of the two of you and memen-
tos of times shared: a tiny cake-top bride to recall
when she helped you pick out your dress; a miniature
airplane to stand for all the flights you've taken to visit
one another; paper umbrellas to symbolize your trip to Hawaii.
Include a letter telling her what you love about her, what you
treasure about your relationship, and what you've learned from
her over the years. Tie the box with a beautiful silk ribbon and present it to her on a special occasion—the anniversary of when you
met or her birthday, perhaps. Or just as a treat out of the blue.

The Eyelash Club

I can't tell you precisely when it started. But sometime in the past twenty-five years, my friend Rose and I developed a little organization called the Eyelash Club. The Eyelash Club is composed of the two of us, who live a thousand miles apart, and is dedicated to discussing everything and everyone in our lives, "down to a gnat's eyelash."

What this means is that we spend hours analyzing not only our own lives and our relationships, but those of each of our friends, and friends of friends. The Eyelash Club tracks the whos, whats, wheres, and whys of dozens of people, many of whom one or the other of us has never met. I know about her friend Sue leaving her job and taking up with a poet in the Midwest; she knows all about my sister's struggles with her novel. She's up to date on the potty training problems my friend Karen is going through; I know all about Fred's sister's breast cancer. On the phone or in person, we check in on one another's circle of friends and family, and through this touching base, we create a network of connection that extends far beyond the two of us. It's not gossip; the talk is to learn, not to judge.

But most of our conversation centers on the two of us—whether she should sell her house, how tired I am all the time, and that perennial female topic: The Men in Our Lives. What should we do next in our lives? What is our growing edge? How can we support one another in doing and being all that we can?

Driving, shopping, having lunch, over tea early in the morning, or late at night, we're talking, talking, talking. No corner of our lives goes unexamined, no minute feeling unremarked upon.

We used to do it as a matter of course whenever we got together. But at some point along the way we institutionalized it. "Let's get together soon and eyelash," she'll say. Or I'll call and request a meeting because "the eyelashes are piling up." Many women keep a journal to track their emotional and spiritual growth. We have the Eyelash Club.

—*M. J. Ryan*

The best mirror is an old friend.

—GEORGE HERBERT

Attraction of Opposites

She is a computer whiz. I'm a computer idiot. She is a gourmet cook. "Cook" is a four-letter word in my vocabulary. She can garden and sew. I uproot flowers and throw away socks with holes. She has a toolbox and can fix almost anything. I'm missing a few screws and can break almost anything.

My best friend and I don't have a lot in common, and yet, wonder of wonders, she is still my best friend. I've often wondered why this is. After all, in high school and college all my friends shared similar passions with me. Not so with Kerri. In many ways, we're opposites. I can draw cartoons and pictures. She's pretty good at coloring. I am often loud and outgoing. She is often shy and reserved. I hold deep religious convictions. She visits church twice a year. I like to exercise every day. She considers vacuuming exercise. How did we end up as such good friends when we are so very different?

Perhaps it's because no matter how many mistakes I make or how goofy I act, she never judges me or ridicules me. Or perhaps it's because when I need help or encouragement, she is right there by my side. I can count on her. She is my number one cheerleader, my listening ear, the second-mom to my kids, the last minute babysitter, and the one who keeps me on my toes. She knows me well enough to anticipate what I might say or do in any given situation. She has already seen me at my worst and hasn't run away screaming.

Perhaps it's all of these things, but I think it may be one simple thing, really. She lets me be me . . . and, well, there's just something special about that.

—*Lori Z. Scott*

Best friend, my well-spring in
the wilderness!

—GEORGE ELIOT

The Surprise Gift

For years now, my wife and I have sent out a Christmas photograph of our four children, along with a family letter and a funny quote from each of our kids. Unbeknownst to us, our best friends Connie and Ed had saved all of our Christmas pictures from all these years, and last year they took each one, had it copied, and presented us with a large, round Christmas-like wreath with a collage of all the pictures inside.

It's just wonderful. As you can imagine, it tells the story of the growth of the four children. We keep it near our front doorway year-round, and guests—and the kids—look at it frequently and start asking questions or remembering things about when the pictures were taken.

—*Tim Schellhardt*

Personalized Calendars

A personalized calendar is perfect for that busy friend who needs to be reminded that you care. Find a wall calendar or make one on your computer. Record all important dates. For birthdays and anniversaries, remember to include the year, such as the person's age or which wedding anniversary it is. You can include fun facts such as the day you graduated from college together, the dog's birthday, and so forth. Use stickers or stamps to denote special days. You can make this really special by scanning in photos (of you two, kids, spouses, etc.) and printing them out to be used at the top of the calendar, with the date grid on the bottom half.

Life is short and we have never too
much time for gladdening the hearts of
those who are traveling the
dark journey with us.

—HENRI-FRÉDÉRIC AMIEL

Photo Swapping

Do you have old pictures your friends would like copies of? It's easy to have them duplicated, even if you can't find the negative. You can scan them and print them out, have them photocopied in color, or use the reproduction services of a good photo shop.

Don't I Know You?

Over the years, I've roamed the United States, moving from job to job. I would make tight friendships and then, before I knew it, I was pulled away on another adventure. Promises of keeping in touch were always made, but phone numbers and addresses would change, and eventually the connection would be lost.

One summer I met a girl named Sandi. We worked together cocktailing at a bar on the beach in Pensacola. It seemed as if we had known each other for years. When the summer ended, she moved back to Wisconsin and I returned to Colorado. At first the distance didn't stop our friendship, but then I received one of my letters back with a notice that she was no longer at that address, and I was devastated.

Many years later, accompanying my husband to a work meeting, I found myself in St. Paul. I had never been anywhere in Minnesota. One evening we were at a restaurant with a group of my husband's cohorts, sipping martinis and looking at the menu. The waitress was sweet and knowledgeable, and there was something very familiar about her mannerisms. We had been there about a half hour when I decided she had a Wisconsin accent. Over the years, with all of my travels I had learned to pick up on different accents. Then it clicked. I looked her in the eye and said, "What is your name?"

Her reply was exactly what I expected, "Sandi."

"You lived in Pensacola," I said.

She slowly nodded yes. I could see her surprise as she stared at me, searching to place my face.

I said, pointing to my chest, "It's me, Beth." Her eyes grew big. We said in unison, "You look so different."

I was so excited I jumped out of the booth, and when I did, a cobalt-blue glass of water crashed to the ground. "I am so sorry!" I said, hugging my long-lost friend.

Throughout the evening we played catch-up, picking up right where we left off. We gave my husband's coworkers a laugh as we told stories of our days together on the beach. We found that Sandi and I both had returned to school and that while I was traveling the U.S., she had been traveling the world.

The excitement of running into someone so dear to me was indescribable. What was even more exciting was realizing I had a second chance at a friendship that I thought was gone forever. In the intervening years, we had both learned how hard true friendship is to come by. We accepted this reunion as a gift and promised not to lose touch again.

—*Elizabeth L. Blair*

We can never replace a friend.

—FRIEDRICH VON SCHILLER

A Magical Lunch

You're sitting down to lunch with your best friends, under an old wooden trellis in the dappled sun. Grapevines with their large veiny green leaves offer shade, their rough old bark trunks telling of years of buttressing the trellis. Jasmine tangles through, starry white flowers perfuming the air. It's pleasantly warm, and an occasional breeze through the lawn sprinkler system brings a cooling current.

This is a moment to treasure, friends once all together now reunited from far distant places. Smiles, kisses hello, the exclamations over children gained and weight lost pepper the air, punctuated by the clink of glasses. Burbling gently as a brook is the background laughter of children, another generation finding soul mates, daring each other to run under the sprinklers, or sneak another slice of fairy cake.

The table is covered in your brightest crockery, with wine and beer glasses, already only half-full glowing ruby red and frosty amber in the sun. Baskets of bread waft crusty warm smells towards you, accented by the acid tang of vinegar and oil dipping sauce.

The compliments flow, and as the afternoon wears on, the laughter grows, old arguments are refreshed, and even older stories are retold. How many times have these stories been told? And with each telling a layer of memory and love is added, until they have the glossy patina of a cherished antique, passed on until the origin is lost.

Full and content, you sit back in your chair, watching the happy faces of your friends, and realize that this is a perfect moment in time, a moment to cherish forever, shared with the people you love best. Life doesn't get any better than this.

—Cindy Tomamichel

Friendship is one of the sweetest
joys of life.

—CHARLES SPURGEON

Bouquet Garni

Bouquets garnis are herb bundles used in many soups and stews. They are great homemade gifts for any cook friends you have.

1 bunch parsley

1 bunch thyme

handful of bay leaves

cheesecloth

white string

Clean, stem, and chop the parsley and thyme. Break the bay leaves into pieces. Combine three parts chopped parsley, two parts chopped thyme, and one part broken bay leaves in a bowl.

Cut out circles of cheesecloth 3½ inches in diameter. Put two heaping teaspoons of the herbs into the center of each circle. Gather up the cheesecloth around the herbs and tie in little bundles with white string. Store in an airtight container. Depending on the size of the bunches, this should be enough for 5 or 6 bouquets garnis.

Sadie Hawkins Day

I was squinting into the video camera, our eight year old rounding bases, when I noticed the limp. No one could have known when our son Vincent began to favor one leg, or that his strained gait was the first sign of fibrodysplasia ossificans progressiva (FOP), a rare genetic disorder that turns muscle into bone. No one could have known that FOP would go on to prevent Vincent from tying his shoes, or that that mild spring afternoon in the San Joaquin Valley marked our son's last season of sports.

We have lived with FOP for years now, hoping for miracles at the University of Pennsylvania's FOP Lab. And we pray for an ordinary life for our son. Though the pain of loss persists, this loss throws life's simple acts of friendship into sharp relief:

Last year, Vincent was invited to his first Sadie Hawkins dance by Clemencia, a pretty brown-eyed freshman. They bought matching camouflage khakis to wear. The morning of Sadie's, the phone rang. It was Clemencia's mother: Her daughter had the flu.

Vincent quietly retreated to the computer. Our son Brian left for a friend's to dress for the dance, and our son Lucas left for basketball. Happy for the others, my throat tightened for Vincent. But the sky was so clear and blue, so my husband, Walt, announced, "We're going to the park to feed ducks!"

"No, thanks," Vincent retorted.

"Come on," called Walt, leading out our daughters, Celine

and Isabel. He extended the invitation again. Vincent refused. From the door, Walt asked again.

"O.K." said Vincent. "But I'm staying in the car."

Our little girls had just started flinging bread at the ducks patrolling the lake, when a swarm of seagulls began to loop and dive furiously for every crust, setting off a group laughing fit. Walt ran to the car to just drag Vincent over for the distraction.

I could see my son's legs swing out stiffly from the passenger's side. A girl in sweats was running past. She stopped.

Vincent and the girl talked. The girl jogged off. And when he got to the lake, Vincent's face was radiant. He had just run into a friend from school, who asked if he was going to the dance. When she heard about his date's flu, the friend invited him to join her large group. Vincent wore his khaki camouflage gear to the dance, and that night, instead of an awkward couple's pose, he brought home a picture of himself in the center of a crowd of friends.

Vincent never goes to this park, one on the other end of the city, far from his Catholic high school. The girl who jogged by

lives in another town. The school itself is a freeway drive away from our home. Up until Sadie Hawkins day, he had never run into a classmate by chance. "Vincent is surrounded by angels," I said that afternoon. And then Walt told me the name of the girl who jogged by at just the right moment: ANGELICA.

—*Carol Zapata-Whelan*

Friendships multiply joys and divide grief.

—Thomas Fuller

The Pleasure of Their Company

Anaïs Nin, in the first volume of her *Diary,* said about friendship that "each friend represents a world in us, a world possibly not born until they arrive. . . ." and in midlife, I have certainly learned the truth of her statement. One of the riches of being midlife women is the ripening and maturing of our longstanding friendships as we realize, perhaps for the first time, how much we depend on their support and help.

We can be totally honest with the friends we've known forever, because they've shared our triumphs—the birth of a child after ten years of trying, unexpectedly swift promotions in a "male" field, an art exhibit at the local library. They've also shared our tragedies—another cross-country move, illness, a child's failed marriage. They listen compassionately and never mention when they've heard our stories before. Sometimes they tell us what to do; sometimes they just lovingly watch with us. They know what we need, often before we do. They bring out our unexpected talents and unsuspected capabilities by believing in us. They reflect us and protect us. They make life worth living.

—SuzAnne C. Cole

You meet your friend, your face
brightens—you have struck gold.

—KASSIA (FIRST-CENTURY BYZANTINE POET)

ABOUT THE EDITOR

SUSANNAH SETON is the editor of *Simple Pleasures, Simple Pleasures of the Home, Simple Pleasures of the Garden, Simple Pleasures of the Holidays*, and *365 Simple Pleasures*. She lives in Berkeley, California, with her husband and daughter.

TO OUR READERS

Conari Press, an imprint of Red Wheel/Weiser, publishes books on topics ranging from spirituality, personal growth, and relationships to women's issues, parenting, and social issues. Our mission is to publish quality books that will make a difference in people's lives—how we feel about ourselves and how we relate to one another. We value integrity, compassion, and receptivity, both in the books we publish and in the way we do business.

Our readers are our most important resource, and we value your input, suggestions, and ideas about what you would like to see published. Please feel free to contact us, to request our latest book catalog, or to be added to our mailing list.

Conari Press
An imprint of Red Wheel/Weiser, LLC
P.O. Box 612
York Beach, ME 03910-0612
www.conari.com